RUNNING

INTO THE

RAINBOW

Barbara and Dale,
Blessed to have had
both of you as part of
our journey. Many Blessings!
Stephanie Wilson

By Stephanie K. Wilson

Jason Wilson

Disclaimer: The contents in this book depict the personal experiences of the author and her family, and are based on her recollections. While the stories recollected include a medical history, it is meant as anecdotal and it should be noted that none of it is to be taken as medical advice. To learn more or obtain a diagnosis, please visit a physician.

This book is a labor of love. I dedicate this book to my beautiful family who has blessed me on this journey through the years. To my husband Scott, who has stuck by me through all the struggles and tears, I could not have done this without you. To my son Dylan who has always been his brother's keeper, I couldn't have asked for a better son or big brother for Jason. For my daughter Kimberly who joined us later in the journey, thank you for devotion to your "little brother." To my incredible parents who have gone over and above to help us on this unexpected journey, thanks for all you do! Last but not least, to my son Jason who literally changed the course of my entire life, I am so thankful that God chose me to be your mom. I love you all more than you will ever know!

'Cause even in the madness

There is peace

Drownin' out the voices

All around me

Through all of this chaos

You are writing a symphony

A symphony

Lyrics from the song *Symphony*
from the band Switch

Table of Contents

Preface

As I sit down to write this, I realize this is a story I never wanted to tell. So many things have happened recently though, that I realize that I have a responsibility to share my story. Even my husband Scott has repeatedly told me that I need to write this down and give it to every person that I meet. He may secretly have an agenda to shorten my phone conversations with complete strangers, but at the end of the day, I know he is right. I have shared my journey in bits and pieces through the years with various people and each time, I realize how this story had the possibility to change the course of someone's life. Mind you, I don't say that lightly. The more time goes on, the more I realize that this story of the journey of my son Jason, as well as my own journey, is important. Other than sitting down with me for hours or getting me on the phone, there is no way you will ever know anything about it unless I sit down to type it out.

Before we begin, I want to premise this by saying that I am "just a mom." That's right! No big credentials. At one point in my life journey, I earned the right to have L.E. after my name, which stood for Licensed Electrologist, and I also held a cosmetologist license. When I say "just a mom," it is not to belittle my experience, but it is to let you know that my lifetime experience as a mom for the past 23 years is what I speak about. As a mom, I have played many roles through the years, and the past almost 18 years have included lead researcher in our family, in order to better understand and help my youngest son.

It is quite a daunting task to bring up 18 years of experiences and put them down on paper in a way that is meaningful and helpful. Just a couple hours ago, I had another call from a parent of a 4-year old son who was given my name by someone I honestly don't even know. I'm sure I have had the opportunity to meet whoever referred them to me somewhere, but to be honest, at this point in my life, I meet new people almost every day (and I have a hard enough time remembering what day of the week it is to get the garbage cans out), so hopefully people will forgive me if I don't remember them the first couple times we meet. I do have an uncanny ability to remember their children though, so if I see them together, I am more able to possibly recall who they are.

Today is the first day of summer vacation. My youngest son, Jason whom you will learn so much about, just graduated high school 4 days ago. Normally, for many parents, this would be a time of great excitement in life, of looking at colleges or military choices. Instead, just last night Jason was asking if the bus is coming to pick him up this morning. (His exact words "bus early up?") For him, even though he just went through weeks of graduation practice and the official graduation last week, along with the obligatory graduation party, he does not understand that school is officially over, at least temporarily. In two weeks, he will actually return to high school for three weeks of half day instruction to help him from regressing over the summer. We aren't concerned with him losing the ability to do algebraic calculations or recalling modern history, we are concerned with him forgetting how to spell his name correctly or possibly start writing his letters incorrectly. Not normal concerns for an almost 18-year old, but definite concerns for Jason who lives with an autism spectrum disorder (ASD) diagnosis.

At the end of summer, he will return to his high school to start the next four years of classes that will be primarily focused on life and job skills. Jason has been in therapy or school since the age of around 15 months and, for him, his journey of education and life skills will continue for many more years.

It is my hope that by sharing our experiences, it may help other parents out there who are going through similar experiences. Get ready, because you are about to go on an eighteen-year journey with me.

Chapter 1

An Unexpected Journey

Birth and the first pediatrician

Here officially begins my story, one which I have shared so many times with people including numerous doctors, throughout the years. In the beginning, I actually typed out a 1 ½ page recap of pertinent medical facts to hand to each new doctor, allowing them read it, so I did not have to retell the same series of events over and over. Now begins the tough part for me, much like the reopening of old wounds. I just pulled out the binders, folders, and envelopes full of Jason's documented journey that brought him to where he is today. As I sit here at my messy kitchen table, cluttered with not only all my documentation, but also an assortment of brand new crayons, some scribbled on paper, graduation envelopes, cards and of course Jason's shoes and toys on the floor around me, I will attempt to document the journey that has gotten us to this point in time.

I realize you most likely don't know me, but to give you a little perspective, I tend to be a little on the OCD side. It would absolutely be my preference to write this story only once my house is cleaned and I could spare looking around at all the clutter that surrounds me at the moment. Given the fact that it is the first official day of summer vacation, though, I know the only time my house will be in my desired state would be after I ship Jason across the neighborhood to his grandparent's house, and then spend hours cleaning only to have it look like this again within an hour of his return. Instead, I'm going to do the best I can, given my current circumstances, which also include listening to Jason burp loudly while watching yet another YouTube video of someone doing something that catches his interest. At least for the moment it is something different than the same song he has played over and over the past few days.

Now, on to our story.

It was the year 2000, and I was working full time at as an administrative assistant to the Director of Quality and Engineering at a semiconductor facility in Camas Washington. I was so excited to land the job there because I could literally see my work off in the distance from my home. I had about a two-minute commute to work and, if I needed to, I had plenty of time to run home at lunch. It was while working there that I found out I was pregnant with my second child. My firstborn son, Dylan, was four years old at the time and by the time Jason arrived into this world; Dylan was just a few months away from starting kindergarten.

Life was good! My husband had a full-time job as an aircraft mechanic at FedEx just across the river in Portland Oregon, and my parents and in-laws had both recently moved up to Washington state. We had a just built a new house, which, at the time, was my dream home, and my parents built their house right behind ours. My in-laws were in the process of building their house next door to ours while living with us. We jokingly referred to our little section of the neighborhood as "the Compound". That was a wonderful time; we had both sets of parents close by and a very sweet son for them to spoil. Within our first couple years there, my middle brother, Frank, also decided to move from California to our town with his family. We went from being completely on our own to being surrounded by lots of family. To top it off, since we lived in a new community, we knew almost every neighbor in the entire neighborhood. Little did we know how much we would need their help in the years to come.

I told you that I was going all the way back to the beginning and that includes the time before I even realized I was pregnant. You see, I went in for a routine dental cleaning and the dentist had determined that one of my old fillings needed to be replaced. It wasn't a big deal; they removed the old mercury filling and replaced it with a new composite filling. I went right back to work after my appointment. I was starving, so I didn't wait until the numbness had completely worn off, instead I awkwardly ate a sandwich at my desk. Unfortunately, I accidentally bit my lip once while still numb and within 2 days, my lip was definitely infected. Again, no big deal, I called my dentist and he called in a prescription for an antibiotic for me. Once I started taking that, my infection began to heal quickly. Two days into taking that antibiotic, I found out I was pregnant. We had only began trying for less than 2 months, so it came as a little of a surprise. Right away, I was concerned about taking the antibiotic and I called my dentist. The dentist switched the antibiotic to amoxicillin, which was supposed to be safe to take while pregnant.

As pregnancies go, my second pregnancy went very well. Sometime that Fall, my employer was offering free flu shots for all their employees. I had never had a flu shot before and, honestly never really remember ever having the flu. It seemed like a good thing to do, so without much thought, I got the flu shot along with many of my fellow coworkers. I do remember actually feeling mildly ill the few days after. Since I was pregnant, I was very limited on any medicines that were safe to take, so I just for the most part had to suffer through it. I can say that I have never since gotten the flu shot and as far as I can recall, I have never gotten the flu. The vague memory of feeling ill after that shot was enough for me to realize that the shot seemed to cause me to be sick when I had been well before.

Little by little, my baby grew. I remember by around 4 months along no longer being able to fit into my regular clothes. I definitely grew much faster this second pregnancy than with the first. The pregnancy was totally normal though, and I was very excited to welcome this new baby into our family. We chose to not find out the gender of either of our babies so we always had a surprise to look forward to at their birth. I had a former coworker whose doctor gave her the incorrect gender with each of her two pregnancies, so I figured I'd rather wait to find out than be told and have the chance that it was not correct.

Overall, my pregnancy was very normal. I did have really bad heartburn towards the end which made it more difficult to eat. I gained a healthy 26 pounds with my pregnancy. I also had extremely itchy hands towards the end. The doctor suggested taking Benadryl, which I did take. I honestly don't recall it helping too much, so the itchiness was something I just had to endure. Overall though, this pregnancy was pretty easy and we were excited to welcome our new baby into the world.

My due date came and, low and behold, later that day, I went into labor. It was nowhere near as painful the second time around. We headed to the hospital and I was admitted right away. I had planned on getting an epidural just like my first pregnancy, and, because of the lack of severe pain that I experienced the first time around, I actually considered skipping it. I then had the thought that I would be crazy to wait until the pain got unbearable like my first pregnancy, so I opted for the epidural. Our baby seemed to be in no particular hurry to be born, but I was comfortable, so I waited patiently. Sometime during my labor, they noticed our baby's heartrate was a little slow, so they gave me oxygen. Nothing seemed too concerning at the time, though, and before I knew it, it was time to push. The doctor was actually still in the cafeteria finishing his coffee when the nurse called him and told him to come to the room. He advised her to have me start pushing and he would be on his way shortly. I did tell the nurse that I pushed out my first baby in 10 minutes, but she didn't seem to think it would be an issue to push without the doctor present.

Guess what? One big push and his head was already coming out! At that point, the nurse told me NOT to push and, she called the doctor and told him he needed to hurry up because this baby was about to come out. Before I knew it, the doctor was there and pretty much by the next push, he was out. I remember them mentioning that his umbilical cord had a knot in it, but it was nothing that would have caused any issues.

June 16th, 2001 Jason Christopher Wilson was born into this world and I couldn't be happier to be the mom of two sons! Jason was born at 8 pounds, 9.5 ounces and had a full head of hair. Dylan, our oldest was so proud to be a big brother.

I think we spent one night in the hospital after Jason was born and then we were already headed back home. Jason was a beautifully perfect baby boy who early on was so much easier to care for than his big brother had been. He did have some jaundice that we noticed, but his brother Dylan had also had a little jaundice at birth and, since the doctor wasn't concerned, we weren't either. Unfortunately, that turned out to be a huge mistake on the part of the doctor.

When I look back at the notes that were in Jason's file at the pediatrician's office, the first notation was from 6/22/01. The notes stated that Jason was 5 days old, but if you do the math, he was actually 6 days old. The notes stated that I was calling because I was concerned that, despite having Jason stripped down to a diaper in a sunny location as much as possible, he still appeared to be very jaundiced. I actually have a picture of Dylan holding him at this time and it is shocking to see how much color Jason had compared to his brother.

In the notes, the doctor ordered a bilirubin test and said to put our son by the window as much as possible and give him an ounce of

Pedialyte every 3 hours. We did the bilirubin tests and the first test they did had his level at a 19.8. This was done when Jason was 6 days old. The following day, they tested him again and his level had dropped a little to 19.1. Because the level had dropped, Jason's doctor was not concerned. She told me that they normally don't put the babies under the lights unless they are at a 20 or above. Keep in mind, at this point, I was having Jason stripped down in a diaper in a sunny window for several hours a day, and he was still this high. Unfortunately, at the time, I completely trusted my doctor and did not push for a second opinion. I had no idea that she made a huge mistake that would cause my son permanent injury.

What I didn't know at that time was that even 3 days of having a bilirubin level 15 or above cause a condition called kernicterus, which is basically brain damage caused by high of levels of bilirubin. That damage is what causes cerebral palsy. I had no idea at the time that my little baby's brain was slowly being damaged, all while I thought I was taking good care of him under the care of his doctor.

Somewhere around the 10th day of Jason's life, he started changing. He no longer was that super easy baby that I brought home from the hospital. Instead, my baby boy would scream about 12 hours a day, almost without stopping. I would try everything and the only thing that occasionally would quiet him down was if I put him in his car carrier on top of a running clothes dryer. Other than that, he rarely slept, and spent most of his time screaming. I still remember some of my amazing neighbors coming over and taking him for walks in his stroller just to give me a break from the constant screaming. He would still scream in the stroller, but they took him for walks regardless.

Having already had one child, I was aware that all babies develop at their own pace. For Jason though, he seemed to scream most of the time from the age of 10 days to around 4 months old. During that time, he did not reach any of the normal baby milestones that most babies develop. I remember being concerned, but the doctor assured me he was fine. At around 2 weeks of age, Jason received his first Hep B vaccine, with his next one about 6 weeks later. At 2 months old, he also received the DTap, Hib. IPV (Polio) and PCV (pneumococcal) vaccines. When Jason received these vaccines, he still had some yellowish color to his skin and eyes, but once again, the doctor showed no concern.

During this time, our pediatrician had discovered that Jason had a heart murmur. She sent him to a cardiologist just to make sure that it wasn't anything serious. As I read through the medical summary from that doctor, it blows me away how they referenced Jason's high bilirubin levels before leaving the hospital, as well as in the weeks that preceded that appointment. In the notes, the cardiologist did reference the possibility of direct hyperbilirubinemia and suggested he be retested to check his bilirubin levels. Five days later, Jason was given his final bilirubin test and he had a bilirubin level of 3.5. Again, only being a mom and not a doctor, I had no idea that that number was a red flag that was once again missed. I also question looking back why my son was given vaccines when his liver function was definitely compromised. Unfortunately, those weren't questions I knew to ask all those years ago.

During this same period of time, the events of September 11th, 2001 happened. I remember that time period so well. Jason was still sleeping in a cradle next to my bed when I quietly turned on the TV to watch the morning news. The first images I saw were of a plane flying into one of the World Trade Center buildings. I couldn't believe my eyes and ran downstairs to call my husband, Scott, who was working across the river in Portland, Oregon. I had no idea about the 2nd plane yet or that the towers were going to collapse. When he answered and told me there was a second plane, I turned on the downstairs TV to watch the horror and reality of what had just happened.

That day really changed so many things in our country so fast. I remember being so scared for the future for my two boys. I'm sure most people who lived through that time period have their own stories to tell. I just remember being so thankful to have my family close by. For at least a little while, my mind was taken off of my daily concern for what was going on with Jason and refocused on what the future would hold for both my boys.

Chapter 2

Next doctor and more concerns

Around the age of 5 months old, our insurance changed, and with that, we also switched to a new pediatrician who took our plan. I wasn't overly attached to our first pediatrician anyway, since she never seemed to take any of my concerns too seriously. I was hopeful that this new doctor would be just what Jason needed to help him get back on track. The screaming that had begun so early on finally started to subside around 4 months of age. I remember thinking at that time that finally my sweet baby boy could start reaching some milestones. In the grand scheme of things, I knew that if he was only 4 months behind, eventually that 4 months wouldn't be a big deal.

Jason was a super cute baby. He had a full head of hair at birth and as time went on it kept growing and getting lighter. I used to spike it up in all different directions, since that is what it wanted to do naturally anyway. At this point in his life, I was still breastfeeding. He did seem to spit up a lot, but I know lots of babies spit up in the beginning so I wasn't overly worried yet.

When we met with the new doctor for the first time, he didn't seem concerned that Jason hadn't reached his normal milestones yet. He gave me the standard talk that all babies are different and, even though my first son did everything on time, there was no reason to believe Jason wouldn't eventually catch up. We went about the normal business of well-baby checkups with all the routine vaccinations that come with those.

As I look back on the notes that the doctor submitted at each visit, it was very clear he was just going through the motions. For each visit, from 4 months and 28 days old to his 6-month visit and even 9-month visit, all the boxes were marked as if Jason was progressing as he should. Unfortunately, Jason wasn't doing any of those things. In the 4-month notes, he marked that Jason could roll over, sit with support, bear weight on legs, babble, blow raspberries, etc., but the reality was that at that point, Jason could only sit in his baby bouncer, so much so that his head was flattening out in the back. Visit after visit, all those boxes were marked as if nothing was wrong. I had no idea until requesting Jason's medical file years later that this was the case. It was just one more case of a doctor, who I was trusting with my son's health, not taking the time to really examine him and listen to the information that I was giving him.

One of my favorite pictures of Jason was taken at 8 months of age. I had planned on having pictures taken at 6 months, like his big brother Dylan, but Jason was not able to sit up yet, so I kept waiting for a better time. At 8 months, Jason could still only sit up with pillows propped around him. It was at that time that he finally had a picture taken. I still remember having to be just out of camera range to help catch him as he would lose his balance and fall back.

Even though Jason pretty much had to live with a bib on all the time because of the spitting up, his doctor again reassured me that this was normal. I had already tried removing all dairy from my diet since I was breastfeeding, but since that didn't help, the doctor suggested to start using formula with rice. At around eight months, Jason didn't seem to be gaining any weight even with the new formula. In fact, he was still spitting up around 50 times a day at that point. I scheduled another doctor appointment because, in addition to still not reaching most of his milestones, he just didn't seem right to me. I still remember so clearly the words of the doctor that day. He told me that our issues were mostly laundry issues, meaning that I just had to do more laundry because of all the spitting up. He also explained Jason's lack of reaching milestones by saying that he was just a "relaxed baby". Seriously! Looking back at it now, it's almost comical the way this doctor dismissed my concerns. Where in all their medical school training had they ever learned that sometimes babies that don't reach milestones are just relaxed! At this point, Jason's height and weight were slowly dropping on the percentile chart, while his head remained toward the top of the percentiles. The doctor sent us home once again with instructions to switch to a different formula and see him again in a month.

With the lack of development and reaching milestones going on, the doctor continued Jason on his routine vaccine schedule. Because we had switched doctors, we were a month behind the normal vaccine schedule, so Jason received his next round at 5 months of age instead of 4 months. The vaccines he received at this time were the DTap, IPV (Polio), Hib (Influenza type b) and the Hep B vaccines. Again, I never thought to question Jason getting vaccines at this time. I fully trusted my doctor to know what was best for my child. After all, they do take an oath to "Do No Harm", so there was no reason for me to second guess our doctor's decision to keep Jason on the normal vaccine schedule.

At nine months, we went back to the doctor to check on Jason's progress. It was at this time that my beautiful baby boy, who was born with a height and weight closer to the top end of the percentile, completely dropped off the chart. Yes, Jason's height and weight were lower than the lowest point on the percentile chart, (considered below zero) while his head was around the 95th percentile. All of a sudden, his pediatrician seemed to wake up to the reality that there was something very seriously wrong with my baby boy. That day put us on a journey of more doctors and tests than I can count. We were sent to see several specialists who were part of the Oregon Health & Science University Hospital, also known as OHSU.

Eighteen years later, upon explaining my son's medical journey to a retired cardiologist, he was completely blown away that so many red flags were being ignored. If you've ever seen pictures of starving children in Africa, with their large heads and tiny bodies, this is what my beautiful baby boy was starting to resemble. He was starving to death right in front of my eyes and the doctors failed to notice until there were no more ways to ignore it.

Chapter 3

Reality Hits Hard

It's one thing when, as a mom, you are concerned that something may be wrong with your child, but it's a whole different ballgame when suddenly your doctor agrees with you. Up until this point, I was concerned and, over time, several family members and friends started to voice their concerns, too. My concerns from that first week of birth until this point always seemed to be explained away by any doctor we saw. Until the doctor finally agreed that something was definitely wrong though, I always held out some hope that maybe there truly was nothing seriously wrong with my baby and maybe his development was really just much slower than his older brother.

This next period of Jason's life started a whirlwind time of visits to specialists, test after test and the start of physical therapy. We did have one huge breakthrough thanks to my cousin who practiced homeopathic medicine in Switzerland. She had the opportunity to meet Jason when he was just a few months old and she stayed in close contact with me regarding his progress or lack there-of. One of our biggest and most pressing concerns was Jason's inability to gain weight or keep his food down. The specialist prescribed Zantac, which we gave him, but saw no improvement. During that time, my cousin asked me many questions to see if she could come up with something to help Jason. When Jason was 11 months old, she sent me some homeopathic medicine which consisted of some tiny pearl like beads that we were to put in his mouth and left to dissolve. She said we could give him the second dose of it in 5 weeks if he needed it. Up until this point in Jason's life, absolutely nothing the doctors had ever done had helped Jason. We gave Jason these little pearls and within 3 days, his spitting up went from about 50 times a day to only 25. Huge progress for him! 5 weeks later, we gave him the second dose and he completely stopped spitting up. Definitely our first victory. To this day, I honestly can't say what those pearls consisted of, all I know is that they gave us our first big step forward in helping Jason finally gain weight and grow.

Sometime during his first year, Jason was also referred to an ophthalmologist to check why his eyes seemed to be off center. He was determined to have pseudostrabismus, but that specialist was concerned about craniosynostosis, so from there, he was referred to a pediatric neurosurgeon for more tests. He also was referred to a Developmental Behavioral

Specialist as well as a Geneticist. With each doctor, we had multiple visits, MRI's, x-rays, blood tests and on and on. I include this just to point out that once, my doctor finally started listening to me, it became very clear to many specialists that there truly was something wrong with my son. If I only had the knowledge back then that I have now, Jason's future may have been much different, but like they say, hindsight is 20/20.

We did have some good news to report during this time, since Jason was finally able to hold his food down, he did start making some progress. At 12 months of age, Jason started having physical therapy at home. We tried everything we could think of to get him moving but had no success. He, at least was finally able to sit up on his own, but that was all he could do. He couldn't scoot or crawl anywhere. I remember never having to worry about leaving him sitting in a room because no matter how long I was away, he would be in the exact same spot when I returned.

Up until this point, Jason never even really babbled like most babies do. Suddenly, Jason surprised us by being able to say full words! I can't begin to tell you how wonderful it was to finally see our baby boy come to life! Jason could very clearly say several words including, kitty, pretty, dada, and his name Jason. I remember finding myself finally taking a sigh of relief. We had been to so many doctors and specialists by this point and, despite their many hours and hours of tests, lab work, MRI's, and x-rays, they had ZERO answers for us. These were some of the top specialists in the Northwest and, their conclusion was that he may end up being one of the 30% of kids that would never have a formal diagnosis.

As a parent, that was a hard pill to swallow. I really wanted answers as to what was happening with my son and why he was so delayed. At least at this point, though, we finally were starting to see him make progress and interact more, so at least it felt like we were on the right track. Unfortunately, within 2 weeks of Jason's well child check-up at 15 months of age, Jason suddenly lost all his words. We noticed it gradually because he had just started speaking that month before. One day it hit us, though, that he wasn't saying any words or making any sounds like he had been. It would be over 3 years of intensive speech therapy, ABA and RDI therapy as well as many treatments and interventions from a naturopathic doctor before we ever recovered any sounds other than crying from our son. To this day, years later, Jason still can't say his name as clearly as he could say it as a baby.

What happened at that well child visit at 15 months that cause our son to regress so much? At the time, we had no idea. All we knew is he went in to that visit with very concrete gains with his height and weight as well as verbal and mobile skills and within a matter of weeks, we seemed to lose him into his own world where he didn't interact with us at all. During that well child visit, Jason received his 4th DTap, his first MMR, and his first chicken pox vaccine. It wasn't until many years later that we began to unravel the mystery of that day.

Chapter 4

Family Life

Part of my reason for writing about Jason and my journey is to hopefully help some of the other families out there who may be at the beginning of their journey into parenthood or maybe just received a diagnosis for their child that they don't know how to process. I think it's important to take a step back right now and talk about what life at home looked like during this first part of our journey with Jason.

It's easy to look at our life all these years later and think that we didn't have it so bad compared to some families, but our journey through the years came with its own set of struggles. I want to mention them just to give other families hope, that even though things may be hard and stressful, you can get through them. Our kids can make huge progress, but it does take time and patience, and the more families can stick together in this journey, the better it can be for everyone involved.

I had mentioned that, when I found out I was pregnant with Jason I was working at a semiconductor company close to my home. I had always dreamed of being a stay at home mom. Our first son, Dylan, was finishing up preschool, and although I occasionally could slip out of work to come join him at special events, it wasn't the same as being there all the time. My husband was still working his way up the pay scale at his job at FedEx. Prior to moving to the Northwest, we had lived in Memphis, Tennessee where he was able to start as an apprentice aircraft mechanic with FedEx. He actually had taken a pay cut when he started working as a mechanic over his previous job as a FedEx courier. We knew that eventually, his pay would increase, and in the long run it would definitely be a well-paying job for him.

Even though I wanted to be a stay at home mom, we couldn't afford to live off of just one income yet. I saw how fast time went by with our first son, and I was determined to find a way to work from home after I had my second baby. I hadn't let my employer know of my plans, or I would have lost out on my maternity leave pay. I had mentioned earlier that we had some great neighbors, well one of them was a realtor, and he offered me a job to work as his assistant from home for 20 hours a week. I was so excited to have this job lined up so I could finally be the stay at home mom that I had always hoped to be.

After my maternity leave ended from my former job, I started working for my neighbor. It was a great job. I would make fliers for his listings, enter information for his listings in the computer, contact clients, schedule showings, the standard stuff that an assistant would do. Having family close by, I had help when I needed it, but as I stated earlier in my story, this was also the part of our journey that Jason was screaming 12 hours a day. Even the loving arms of his Oma and Nana were not enough to soothe him. As much as they wanted to help, Jason became too much to handle for long for them. I tried to work through the crying and screaming when I needed to, but it got to the point that I couldn't answer phone calls or make calls without having a screaming child in the background. This definitely was not the professional environment that was needed to be a good assistant for a successful realtor.

I was heartbroken and stressed. My "perfect" job that I had found to make it possible to be a stay at home mom had turned out to be not so perfect after all. We still needed me to bring in an income though, and it was very clear that if my own mother and mother in law could both not handle watching Jason for long, daycare was definitely not an option. I decided to do the one job where it wouldn't matter if Jason was constantly crying; I started doing childcare from home. One of my former coworkers from the semiconductor company, who actually took over my position after I left my former job, had her baby 3 months after I had Jason. I started watching her son Cameron full time and also watched a little three-year old boy named Hayden, who was the son of my friend and neighbor.

Childcare came with its own set of challenges, but at least I could focus on Jason and the other kids without the stress of having phone calls and computer work to do. As it turned out, Cameron was also a crier. He also hated baths, so much so that his mom often brought him needing one. He was her first child and she couldn't handle his screaming during bath time. I had gotten immune to the screaming by this point, so my mom would come over and help while I would bathe Cameron. You would think we were pouring boiling water over him by the way he reacted to his baths. Fast forward a little further into the future and Cameron would one day be diagnosed with autism. Those baths that he hated, for some reason caused him a huge sensory overload.

As life was going on for Jason's first year, I was running an in-home daycare and relying on my mom's help every time Jason had another doctor appointment. It wasn't easy, but I was truly thankful that I could be there for both my boys. Sometime around the time that Jason was a year old, I also went to a Mary Kay party and low and behold, I ended up signing up to become a Mary Kay consultant. With my cosmetology background from years back, it seemed a good fit at the time to help bring in additional income. I won't go into too much detail, but I did Mary

Kay for about 18 months. I was actually working my way up as a consultant and had a small team under me. Turned out not to be the money maker I had hoped though because I was under water financially with the inventory that I was encouraged to purchase. I can say though that I really enjoyed having a diversion at the time to hang out with women and play with makeup. I also received some incredible training that would serve me well at my next business venture and beyond. I even made it to one of the Mary Kay conventions in Dallas before deciding that Mary Kay was not the right fit for me.

When I look back at those early times, I really wish there would have been someone to talk to, who was going through some of the same things that I was going through with Jason. This was way before Facebook turned into what it is today. All I had was the internet, and I would search for hours to try to find answers to what was going on with Jason. It was on one of those searches that I came across a study from the University of Pennsylvania that showed just 3 days of a baby having a bilirubin level of 15 could cause brain damage. Of course, I found this study way too late to help Jason, but it was the first thing I remember finding that made me realize that my doctor definitely made a mistake in Jason's care. In the years to come, I would spend hundreds if not thousands of hours on the internet researching constantly to try to find answers to how I could help my son.

Having a child with special needs can become pretty overwhelming, especially when you realize that doctors don't have all the answers that you would expect them to have. We have doctors who can figure out how to separate Siamese twins, but I couldn't find any doctor to give me answers on what was wrong with my son. All the doctors could agree on was that something was definitely wrong, and I should get him in physical and speech therapy ASAP.

Chapter 5

The fix-it phase

This next phase of Jason's life I will refer to as the fix-it phase, because I was doing everything I could to fix whatever it was that was wrong with him. Once we exhausted our search for an answer with every medical professional that we possibly go to, we started seeing non-traditional doctors for more help. My life revolved around me constantly searching for answers on the internet and joining parent forum groups, where I would learn that other parents were experiencing some similar things with their kids.

Jason was officially in the system with the Washington State Department of Social and Health Services. He qualified for speech and physical therapy that was taking place in our house. We also were referred to Shriners Hospital in Portland, Oregon, and we began getting services and therapy also with them. In addition, we were also taking him to additional speech therapy that we had to fight to get our insurance provider to cover. You would think speech therapy would be a covered benefit for a child who was not speaking, but it only was covered after several appeals with our insurance.

It was during this time that my mom had mentioned Jason's issues to her chiropractor, Dr. Lewis. He thought he may be possibly able to help Jason, and asked her to have me bring Jason in, and he would do an adjustment on him at no charge. I had nothing to lose, so of course we went to see him. He did do an adjustment, but after his examination, he really thought Jason could benefit by seeing a craniosacral therapist. He consulted with several other chiropractors to help find us the best one in the area. He gave us a name of Dr. Jacque, and he even rescheduled his appointments so that he would be able to meet us at her office, which was about an hour away.

We started seeing Dr. Jacque for several adjustments when Jason was around 14 months old. Before he saw her, he could only sit up if he was propped up by pillows. After his very first adjustment with her, he could finally sit without falling over. His second adjustment helped him to finally get up on his hands and knees, and after his third adjustment, he started crawling! Her work with him gave us such incredible results in terms of finally helping him start to move, but as he grew, he also started fighting his treatments, so there was a period of time that we didn't see her because she didn't want to force treatments on Jason. We waited until Jason was a little bit older to go back to seek more treatments.

I remember so clearly one visit with a genetic specialist from OHSU when Jason was getting closer to 2 years old. Keep in mind, Jason still couldn't walk at this age, but at least he had made progress to start pulling himself up on things. After about 5 minutes of an examination and spending time learning about Jason, I had mentioned to this doctor that I knew one day Jason would be able to walk. Remember, I have now spent almost 2 years of my life seeing my son day in and day out. I knew he was very behind in his motor skills, but I was still seeing progress, no matter how slow it was. This particular doctor with all his wisdom stopped me and said that there was a chance Jason might never walk. Talk about a jaw dropping moment! The thought of Jason not walking had never once entered my mind. I immediately knew that this doctor had no idea what he was talking about, and I was happy to have the appointment end shortly thereafter. What he said though, hit me like a ton of bricks. I knew in my heart he was wrong, and I wondered how many other children he so quickly judged without taking the time to really learn about them. Had I been one of those more impressionable parents, who believed every word their doctors told them, I may have given up on all the extra physical therapies, thinking they were all in vain. Thankfully though, I had already come to the conclusion that doctors did not have all the answers, and I continued with Jason's therapies.

A few months after the appointment where we were told our son may never walk, Jason officially took his first steps on his own. He actually took his first unassisted steps on my mom's birthday, and to this day, she remembers it as being one of her favorite Birthday presents. Jason was almost 25 months old at this point. Because he was already getting so tall, the standard walkers were too short to help him. Instead, Shriners hospital used a kid sized grocery cart to help him balance, as he learned to take his first steps.

I can't begin to explain what a huge relief it was to us to finally see Jason walking. That was our number one goal for him above all else. We knew, that if he were ever able to have a chance at living an independent life, walking would be a critical skill for him to have.

Shortly after Jason mastered walking, we noticed that he tended to mostly walk on his tip toes. Over time, it became an issue that needed to be addressed. Luckily, the Shriners hospital we were going to, specialized in this type of care. Jason was able to have Botox injections to loosen the muscles in his lower legs. After the Botox injections, Jason had to wear plaster casts for a month so the tendons could stretch and he would be able to walk flat footed. After the casts came off, he was fitted with his first of many AFO's (ankle foot orthosis.)

Around the time, we started seeing Dr. Jacque again, we were given the news from a tympanogram (specialized hearing test) that Jason had low frequency hearing loss, along with some high frequency hearing loss. It was with those results that we were given the news that Jason required hearing aids. This was just one more thing that we were prepared to deal with. There was a follow-up tympanogram scheduled, but before we had that next appointment, Jason had an appointment to see Dr. Jacque, his craniosacral specialist. He was going in for an adjustment, but I happened to mention to her that Jason would soon be fitted for hearing aids. Upon hearing this news, she mentioned that she may be able to help by doing an adjustment through the roof of his mouth that could help adjust to bones in his ears. She offered to do the adjustment on me first so I would understand what it would feel like for Jason. I had an issue with one of my ears always feeling a little blocked, so I asked her to do it for my right ear. The procedure made me gag a little because it required her fingers to go close to my throat, but the second she did it, instantly I could feel my ear drain, and the blockage in my ear completely cleared up.

She then performed the same adjustment to Jason for both his ears. He wasn't very happy about it at the time, but it was over within seconds. My mom babysat him shortly after that appointment and she still remembers him almost crawling up the walls because he seemed to be over stimulated by all the new sounds. That next week we went in for his follow up hearing test and, miraculously, Jason's hearing tested to be perfect. It was shocking how well the procedure worked for him. The doctors told us that if we had given him hearing aids at that point, it would damage his hearing. To this day I am incredibly thankful to that one chiropractor, named Dr. Lewis, who took his time to find this specialist for us. Had it not been for him, there would have been the chance that Jason may never have learned how to walk, and he may have had to use hearing aids to hear.

Once Jason started walking, a huge weight was lifted off our shoulders. We knew that he still had so many issues that we needed to deal with, but at this point we could at least know that he would be able to get around on his own. Since every house we lived in had stairs, it sure made life a little easier. Over time though, Jason did become more unstable, as his toe walking got worse. When he would have a growth spurt after his Botox treatments wore off, he would become more unstable and fall more often. Unfortunately for him, he did have a couple bad falls that resulted in visits to urgent care. One of his visits required his head to be glued back together from a fall when his older brother accidentally forgot to lock the extra lock on the front door. Another fall down a few stairs resulted in a broken nose that was too swollen to reset. The doctor suggested bringing him back in a few days after the swelling went down, to reset it. We couldn't bring ourselves to put him through additional pain though after the original injury, so to this day, Jason still has a crooked nose from that fall.

When Jason was 4 years old, we had moved to a neighboring town from where we lived, which meant that he would now be part of a new school district. He had been attending a preschool for special needs children, half days, several days a week, and he transferred to the preschool program in the Camas school district. Keep in mind that during this time Jason still had no speech skills, and he did not interact with people. He lived in his own world, and it was almost impossible to initiate eye contact with him. He also, at times, would randomly slam his head into the hardest object he could find, often the wood floor. He still lacked a formal diagnosis, but by the age of 3, from all my research, I had already come to the conclusion that he had autism. I had given up trying to get answers from any doctor, other than to continue to fight to get him as much physical and speech therapy that I could, and I hoped that the school he was going to could help him make progress.

It was at Jason's new preschool, that we finally got one step closer to receiving a diagnosis. After only two weeks in the classroom, I was called in for a special meeting. His teachers wanted to sit down with me and ask me personally what I thought was going on with Jason. For that question, I had an easy answer based on all my research- autism. They completely agreed with my personal diagnosis, but in the state of Washington, teachers were not able to offer a diagnosis. They recommended I go to our pediatrician and give him all the information of what I observed with Jason. By this time, we were on our 3rd pediatrician since the first two had been completely worthless to Jason and, in my opinion, caused him more harm from their lack of proper medical care.

I made an appointment with Jason's new pediatrician and explained to him everything Jason was doing or not doing. Here was my list:

- Not speaking/loss of speech he did have
- No eye-contact
- Often flapping his arms
- Obsessed with things that would spin, like ceiling fans
- Wouldn't respond to his name or other requests
- Would not play with other children
- Obsessed with anything with strings
- Poor motor skills

Even though we had previously seen this new doctor for a routine visit, he never offered us a diagnosis. Once I gave him all of Jason's background, he completely agreed with me that Jason should be diagnosed with autism. After all those years and so many doctors and tests, it came down to this very simple visit to finally get a real diagnosis. I have to say that I left the appointment that day a little stunned. I hadn't expected for the doctor to actually listen to what I had to say and agree with me. I had been let down so many times along this journey that when I finally had a solid answer, I wasn't sure what to do next.

Finally having a diagnosis for Jason meant that he could start attending school every day instead of just a few times a week. I am so thankful for those teachers at Jason's new school, who took the time to encourage me to speak to my doctor. Other than finally having a name for Jason's condition, not much changed that day. I think a lot of people expect that once they receive a diagnosis that the doctors would have a list of treatments available and also a list of what to do next. Instead, the only thing we left with was a paper from our doctor's prescription pad that gave the diagnosis of autism for Jason. What we did with that information from that point on was fully on us to decide.

One great benefit to Jason's new school was that I was able to meet other moms who had kids with autism. The phrase to describe these moms is commonly referred to as "autism moms." I was invited to join their group where they would meet once a month at a restaurant and talk about a little bit of everything over drinks and appetizers. Even though I had done so much research online, some of the information these moms had, really blew me away. From these moms I learned about additional treatments and therapies. I wanted to do everything and anything to help my son, so I added even more treatments and therapies to his already busy schedule.

When I look back, it's truly difficult to say exactly what it was that helped Jason the most. We were doing everything at once, and we didn't have the luxury of time to just try one thing at a time and see what would work. From about age four to age six, Jason's entire life became a series of treatments and therapies. He was on a gluten and casein free diet, which was very challenging for a boy who loved Pop Tarts and milk. Just finding food he could eat that didn't have wheat or dairy was a job in itself. We also did IV chelation therapy, which helped to remove certain metals his body tested very elevated in. We didn't understand why his body would be so high in these metals, but we did know that we needed to do what we could to get them back to a more normal range. When you do chelation though, it takes out the good and the bad, so Jason also had to take a wide array of supplements to put back in what his body needed.

We also added additional therapies that we would do privately at home. Jason had ABA therapy (Advanced Behavioral Analysis) and also RDI therapy (Relationship Development Intervention). These therapies helped Jason to start to learn the meaning of words and also start to learn how to interact with us. The RDI therapy also definitely helped in teaching Jason to look back, to see if we could see him as he was walking away. Definitely an important life skill that helped eventually break the cycle of him always trying to wander off.

As great as all these therapies and treatments were for Jason, none of them were covered by our insurance. It still blows me away that some of the only treatments that existed at the time that actually were helping my son, were not a covered benefit. I think that autism grew at such an alarming rate, that the insurance companies just couldn't keep up. As a parent, I wanted to do everything possible to help my child, so as we continued on our path to help Jason, our credit card debt started to grow quickly. Having a child with special needs is stressful enough on a family, and adding huge financial debt definitely did not make things any easier.

Chapter 6

Our Final Year in the Northwest

Wow! That last chapter got long and I really only scratched the surface of what was going on during all those years. Remember, Jason also had an older brother who still needed our time and attention too. We used to refer to Dylan as his brother's keeper. We truly could not have asked for a more loving big brother for Jason. It was tough balancing all of Jason's appointments and also making sure Dylan got to enjoy being a kid. I had always dreamed of being a mom, and to be honest, my dreams never included autism, but with Dylan, I got to experience motherhood the way I always hoped it would be. Dylan was just starting Kindergarten a few months after Jason was born, and when I could, I would come and help out in Dylan's classroom.

Dylan truly was a wonderful child, and it was a joy to watch him learn how to ride a scooter and then a bike. He also played T-Ball, soccer, and basketball. We had fun birthday parties for him, and I still cherish the pictures of him with all his little friends.

It was inevitable that Jason's autism would affect Dylan's life; but we really made an effort to make sure that Dylan still had special experiences too. From a very young age, Dylan definitely had a lot more responsibilities to keep his brother safe. Once Jason could walk, it didn't take long for him to learn how to run. It sure was nice to have Dylan around to chase after him for us.

Speaking about running, there is definitely something that Jason started doing once he mastered walking. When he would run, usually he would run with one arm bent up with his hand hanging down. I remember saying he runs like a kid that has cerebral palsy. Through the years, he got better control of his arms, but occasionally he still does raise it in an awkward position when he runs.

Jason, lived in his own world most of the time. The only interaction he seemed to crave was from animals. Once he started making sounds again, the animals were the ones who he tried to talk to. To this day, he can be very silent around people, but if there is a dog or cat nearby, suddenly he starts talking to them. We can't always understand his words, but he truly seems to have a gift when it comes to dogs. They love him because he showers them with love and attention.

As we were about to head into the summer before Jason started kindergarten, I once again was called in for a special meeting at his school, this time with one of the main administrators. Up to this point we were unsuccessful in getting Jason potty trained. All the normal methods that we used with his big brother Dylan had no impact on Jason. Luckily for me, I was given excellent advice that day that to this day, I am still thankful for. Potty training was the next big step to helping Jason live a more independent life. I welcomed any suggestions that could help Jason to be successful. He was in pullups at this point because he no longer fit into diapers. The administrator told me to get rid of the pullups immediately and only use regular underwear with Jason. She said, that until he actually could feel the wetness from having an accident, he would never figure out how to use the toilet. Just like everything else when it came to autism and helping Jason, I was willing to give it a try.

I'm happy to report that it only took one week of accidents for Jason to finally figure out how to use the toilet to go potty. Going poop though, took two months of accidents before we ever had our first success. What a glorious day that was though when Jason finally got it! He was standing next to me in our front living room when a look came across his face and he took off running to the bathroom. Low and behold, he went poop on the toilet for the very first time! What a huge relief! To this day Jason attends school with kids older than him who still have accidents or wear diapers. That day put him on the path to one day being fully potty trained. We did go through a lot of pairs of underwear in the process. Sometimes, if an accident happened when we were out of the house, it was just too messy to keep the underwear, and we would dispose of it. It was so much cheaper in the long run than having to buy diapers for many more years.

By this point at age 5, Jason had accomplished two of our three main goals that we had for him to be able to live a more independent life. He could walk and he could use the toilet. The third goal of being able to speak would not be so easy to reach. What we did know was that our boy, who was in his own world for so long, was slowly able to function a little better in our world.

One thing that seemed to become a theme in our life was keeping Jason safe. He was quick to wander off and disappear, so we had extra high locks installed in our home to keep him from opening doors. Jason went briefly missing on us once at a shopping mall. I thought his father was watching him while I was paying at the register and his father thought Jason was with me in the back of the store. It was a very panicked few minutes of running into stores and asking if people had seen him. Luckily, his father located him several stores down from where we originally were. He was so fast, that for a while we had a cute backpack that had a leash attached, that we would use when we were out in public.

The fear of that day at the mall did not begin to compare to what happened a few months later. We lived in a house on a hill and the main floor of the house was on the second story. Getting to the driveway required us to go down a flight of brick stairs in front of the house. Our morning school routine was that we would go down the stairs with Jason and he would run around the driveway until the bus arrived. Because stairs were still a little difficult for Jason, it would usually take him about a minute to navigate down the stairs to the driveway.

One morning, I was finishing up dishes in the kitchen, when I heard the front door open. I knew Jason was headed down to the driveway, so I quickly put the last dishes in the dishwasher before heading to go wait for the bus with him. Unfortunately, when I went down the stairs to the driveway, Jason was nowhere to be found.

Keep in mind that even when I would call out Jason's name, he would not answer, but

I was calling his name anyway. I couldn't believe he could possibly disappear that quickly on his own. I ran to both ends of our property to look up the hill just in case he wandered in the yard. I realized I had not actually seen him leave the house, I only heard the door open and close, so I quickly ran inside the house for a quick search to make sure he wasn't still inside. My worst nightmare was unfolding before me when I realized he truly was missing. I ran to get my husband who was just about to get in the shower. Within five minutes of first hearing that door open, we were both in our cars going uphill and downhill to see if we could find him. There was no sign of him anywhere!

At this point, I was terrified that he had possibly been kidnapped from our driveway. I didn't see how it was possible for him to disappear so quickly. I called 911, and there was an immediate call put out across the wire for a missing child- mine! I found out later from a friend that there was even something immediately on the radio about a missing five-year-old boy in Camas Washington. As much as I wanted to keep searching, the police dispatcher told me to go back home immediately and an officer would meet me there. Just writing about this experience still brings tears to my eyes. Autism or no autism, I could not begin to imagine my life without my sweet little Jason!

The officer arrived and we gave him pictures of Jason and answered all kinds of questions. It seemed like an eternity and I couldn't stop crying. 30 minutes after the time that Jason was reported missing, a call came across the police radio that he had been found. Jason was having a great time playing on a swing at a park that was at the bottom of our hill. He had never gone there by himself, and he must have taken the shortcut path that ran between two houses, and that would explain why I couldn't locate him when I drove down the hill with my car.

The officer took me in the squad car to be reunited with Jason. We picked up Jason and rode home together in the police car. The events of that day have impacted me for years. Apparently, two weeks before, in the neighboring city, a very similar scenario played out with another young boy with autism going missing. Although that young boy ended up being safely located a few hours later, the nightmare of that day was not over for the family. At that time, autism was still relatively new to most people, police included. The circumstance of their son going missing resulted in CPS being called and their son with severe autism was removed from their home for a week, while the state investigated.

Within about two hours of Jason returning home, we had a visit from the Sheriff's department. Fortunately for us, because of the prior circumstance of the other boy going missing, the department now treated missing children cases a little differently when it involved a child with autism. Instead of having Jason removed from our home and an investigation opened, we were offered something called Project Lifesaver for Jason. Project Lifesaver involved a waterproof GPS device that Jason would wear on his wrist in a special band that could only be cut off. The GPS was trackable by a special device that the Sheriff's office had which could locate Jason within a five-mile radius, even by helicopter.

We were truly thankful that, not only did they understand the situation, but they also offered us a way to help keep Jason safer in the case of him ever wandering off again. His school was well aware of the situation and had been given specific instructions to call the Sheriff's office immediately in the case that Jason ever went missing. About two months after the incident with Jason going missing from home, he did go missing again, but this time from his school. He went to use the bathroom that was just outside of his classroom door, and when the teacher went to check on him, he was nowhere to be found. A call was made immediately to the

Sheriff's Department, but at the same time, several staff members were actively searching for him on the school grounds, and they found him across the street from the school. Once he was spotted, the teacher called out his name and Jason turned around and started walking towards the teacher, into the direct path of an oncoming car! I honestly feel that God sent a special angel that day to watch over my son, because the car stopped in time and Jason was safe once again. The next phone call was to me, to inform me of what had happened. cfaIt all happened so fast that I wasn't informed of the situation until after it was resolved. For that I am truly thankful, because I don't know if I would have been able to handle the emotional turmoil that would have resulted of knowing my son was missing once again.

A few months later, my husband Scott would take a job transfer that would take us to South Texas, far away from family and friends who we held so dear and had grown to rely on. As much as I was looking forward to a sunnier and warmer climate, it was bittersweet leaving all the support behind that we had in the Northwest. Given the current state of our finances and the debt that we had accumulated paying for medical treatments though, this move couldn't have happened at a better time. We were able to sell our house and pay off our debts and move to an area with a much more affordable cost of living.

We moved in the summer, just in time before Jason would start first grade and Dylan would be starting middle school. There was definitely a big culture shock when we arrived. Coming from the Northwest where the population was predominately white, we now lived in an area that was 90% Hispanic. We also did not speak Spanish, which would definitely add to the challenge in our new area. The good news was that, the people in our local community were absolutely wonderful and welcoming. We quickly learned some simple Spanish phrases to help us better communicate with our new friends.

Chapter 7

New Beginnings in Texas

As I continue to write this, I realize it may be a lot of information to take in, especially given that fact that I am only writing about the journey of one child- mine. There are so many small details that happened along Jason's journey though that I believe truly changed the quality of his life. I don't want to leave those details out, because it is truly my hope that what we did to help Jason, may hopefully help other children too.

We moved to an area of Texas that is about as far south as you can go before you hit Mexico. We are about 40 minutes from the Mexican border and 15 minutes from the beautiful beaches of South Padre Island. I'll tell you what, if you are going to have to live with a child with a disability, it sure is a lot nicer to do it on a sunny beach than in a cold rainy climate. Of course, even living in an area that can feel like paradise, at times can also present some challenges.

I still remember as we drove into town in our moving truck, seeing about half the windows in town boarded up. Somehow my husband had convinced me that this part of Texas really wasn't prone to getting hurricanes. What I witnessed as we drove through town that first day definitely made me realize that he may have been a little mistaken. It turned out that there was a hurricane in the Gulf of Mexico that had the possibility of coming ashore in our area. Fortunately, that hurricane diverted to a different direction and we were able to move in without dealing with hurricane force winds. It wasn't until the following summer that we would have to deal with Hurricane Dolly.

The job transfer happened so fast, that we hardly had time to find a house to rent. Luckily, through the miracle of the internet and a coworker of my husband who had transferred to the area the year before, we were able to find a small rental house that was about a third of the size of the house we had just moved out of. It was definitely a tight fit, and most of our belongings stayed packed in boxes in the garage. At least both boys had their own rooms, but they did have to share a bathroom. I always told Dylan to enjoy his big room and private bath while he had it because we wouldn't always live in a house that large. In the Northwest, we moved a few times and each time we were able to flip our houses and make a nice profit. It wasn't until the last house we owned there, the one where Jason went missing, that the market finally took a downturn. We were fortunate to be the only house in the neighborhood to sell in an entire year, and although we didn't really make money on it, we were able to break even after all the taxes and fees were paid. We moved just before everything in the real estate market really crashed and caused many people to go through foreclosure. Given our current state of medical debt that we had prior to the move to Texas, we definitely felt incredibly blessed to not only survive the housing crash, but also to finally be caught up on bills and have a little extra money in the bank.

Not having the financial burdens of a large house and lingering medical debt, definitely simplified life. Jason was taking in his new environment and it was very clear early on that he loved the heat. My last couple years in the Northwest, I had stopped doing childcare and instead became a part time consultant for a direct sales company called PartyLite, where I did home parties for hostesses to help them earn free candles and beautiful accessories. It was something I was able to fit in with all of Jason's appointments and Dylan's activities and definitely proved to be much more profitable than my short time as a Mary Kay consultant. In the first few months of business, I was able to earn my first free vacation to the Atlantis resort in the Bahamas. It was somewhere I had never imagined going and somewhere we would have never been able to afford to go given our current financial state. Over the 8 years that I was a consultant, I was able to earn several free vacations including our favorite, a European cruise out of Barcelona. Those vacations gave my husband and me the opportunity to have a real break from the stress that we lived with every day at home. We were so fortunate to have my parents close by to help with our boys.

I had grown a good size team of PartyLite consultants before we moved and, through the grace of God, I was able to successfully restart my business in my new town where it seemed nobody had ever heard of the PartyLite company. I want to mention this part of my life because my wonderful sponsor Shahna and my incredible team of consultants really helped me to have some normalcy in my life, when so many things seemed out of my control. There was definitely a time where depression hit me. Living in the Northwest, and having something to escape to from the reality of having a special needs child really helped me get through some of the more difficult times. Not only that, but also knowing that I needed to retain a certain level of business to retain the commissions from my team that I had grown, gave me a lot more incentive to step out of my comfort zone and find new ways to grow my business in my new home town.

My husband had his own way of dealing with our situation. For a short time before our move, he started drinking beer more often. We never were big drinkers, but he seemed to go from having a beer in the evening to maybe having two to three beers. Nothing ever can prepare you for the stress that comes from having a special needs child, and I think we both had our own way of coping with it. Although two to three beers might not sound like a lot, for me I started getting concerned enough that I brought up my concerns to him and even though he thought I was over reacting, he did start drinking less.

I have seen many marriages break up among my friends who have kids with autism. It didn't happen overnight, but it did happen often. I honestly could not imagine taking this journey without my husband by my side. Some days, when I feel I had enough, I have been able to rely on him to take over. He truly has been an amazing father for all of our kids (you'll learn of Jason's future sister later) and I am so thankful that our marriage has survived this tough journey.

I wrote in the beginning of wanting to share about our journey and I think it is important to write not only about the successes, but also about the struggles. I am at the point in my journey where I often find myself speaking to people who are just newly coming to terms with the diagnosis of their child. I truly want to be able to help give a little hope and to hopefully help them though some of the difficult times that they may experience.

When we arrived in Texas the summer before Jason was to start first grade, we went to get him registered for school. One of the things the school asked for was his immunization records, which I had. I had mentioned earlier about all the vaccines that Jason received from birth to 15 months of age. We gave him all the recommended vaccines without ever knowing to question if he was having adverse reactions to them. After his last round of vaccinations at 15 months, where he seemed to change so much in such a short period of time, including losing all his newly acquired words, my mother's intuition kicked in and I started to wonder if possibly he wasn't able to tolerate the vaccines like other kids could.

When it came time for his next round of vaccinations at age 4, we were already on our third pediatrician. I discussed my concerns with him and he agreed with my observation that Jason had adverse reactions to prior vaccines. Due to that discussion, the decision was made to not give him additional vaccines.

Now that we were in a new state though, the school district urged me to take him to a doctor here and see about getting vaccines. When I met with the doctor and discussed Jason's medical history, they understood my concerns regarding giving him further vaccinations. They did strongly urge me to consider giving him the Hepatitis A vaccine though, because we were so close to the Mexican border. My job as a mom, is to do the best job I can to keep my child healthy and I know that there is a risk to Jason's health if I vaccinated him and there also could be a risk to his health if I didn't. There was no easy answer, but I took the risk of giving him this one more vaccine, in the hopes of helping prevent Hepatitis A. Unfortunately for him, he had horrible diarrhea for 3 months following this vaccination. When it came time a year later for his booster shot of the Hepatitis A vaccine, I let the doctor know about what happened with him the year prior and they agreed with me that he definitely had a vaccine reaction and that we should no longer vaccinate.

I was able to apply for a vaccine waiver through the Texas Department of State Health Services to opt out of future vaccines for Jason. That was the only form the school needed for him to enroll. It actually didn't matter why we made the decision not to vaccinate, as long as we turned in a new form every 2 years, he was able to attend public school.

Given the fact that Jason had a history of wandering, I was very concerned to have him start school in a new town where nobody knew him at all. I let the school administrators know of Jason's history prior to our move and also asked if they had the project lifesaver program in their town. I was very disappointed to hear that they did not. I think I scared them enough with the accounts of Jason going missing in the past, and the close call with almost being hit by a car, that they made the decision that Jason would have a one to one aid with him at all times. Jason also needed a one to one to help him learn because he could become distracted very easily. For me, it definitely put my mind at ease, knowing that there was someone assigned to be with him at all times.

I have to be honest, I had huge reservations about moving to such a small town in terms of what the quality of the schools might be like. Our school district has such a high number of students who are classified at the poverty level, that every single student gets free breakfast and lunch every day. My boys with their fair skin from the Northwest definitely stood out a little among their fellow classmates. It took about a year of living here before I stopped noticing how much we all stood out. It definitely was a culture shock in the beginning, but as time went on, we have really grown to love this community.

I am happy to say that we were pleasantly surprised at how much we liked this new school district. Jason's teacher and his paraprofessionals were wonderful with the kids, and they definitely seemed to really do their best to give them opportunities to learn and also participate in school activities. Jason had a special group of four other students that he started with in first grade and stayed with his entire 12 years of school. Through the years, this beautiful group of kids has been lovingly given the name of the Fab Five. Although they have also added other older and younger classmates to their group of friends through the years, this group has always had a special bond.

We really started to enjoy life in our small town and Jason was adjusting to a very different life. Prior to moving, Jason spent so much time after school attending various therapies and appointments. That was the time period I refer to as our "fix it phase". It's almost as we lived life in a panic mode of realizing something was wrong with Jason, and we knew we needed to fix it before it became permanent. Jason was so severely affected by autism in those early years and I am truly grateful that we were able to help him become more engaged in our world and not so distressed all the time. At the same time though, we knew that financially we couldn't afford to keep up with the pace of what we had been doing, and we found out the hard way that there were almost no special services available in our area, even if we did have the financial resources to pay for them.

At the end of the day, we had to make a decision in regards to Jason. If we really wanted him to be in an area where there were more therapies and options for naturopathic doctors available, we would need to consider moving again. We also knew that we couldn't ever again go that far into debt paying for medical expenses, because we wouldn't have the option of selling a house to help us pay off the bills. We made the decision to let Jason enjoy just being a kid and instead we would do as much as we could as his family to engage him in play and help him to learn from us. The only therapy he would receive would be given during his school time. For us as a family, this was the right decision.

Over time, we were able to introduce different foods back into Jason's routine. The first things that we were able to add back were gluten products like bread and cereal. There were times, where just a small amount of that type of food would trigger more behaviors in Jason, but as his body began to heal from the inside, he was able to start eating these foods again without any adverse effects. Milk was the very last thing that we slowly added back into his diet, because it seemed to affect his stomach more. Over time though, he could also tolerate milk again, which definitely made life much easier since he always had access to it at school.

With no more appointments and therapies, we finally had time to enjoy just being together as a family. We loved going to the beach and Schlitterbahn, the local water park. For Jason, everything took time for him to get used to. The first year we were here, we had to carry him on to the beach, because he was not used to walking on sand. We would carry him and then set him on a towel and slowly, he started realizing that he enjoyed playing with the sand. Jason was also terrified of going in the swimming pool. We had a neighborhood pool that we would go swim in and Jason would only walk around the pool and occasionally sit next to the pool to get his feet wet. If anyone came near him though, we would run off because he was afraid to go into the water.

At the Schlitterbahn waterpark, we would put him on a double tube with us. His section had a plastic bottom, so he wasn't actually touching the water. Often, in the beginning, he would cry when we took him. Back then, he was still little though, so we could just pick him up and put him in. The turning point for Jason, in terms of going in the water, happened when he for the first time felt the warm water in the swim up bar at Schlitterbahn. We explained to him that it was just like a giant bathtub, and somehow those words made sense to him, and he finally started to enjoy the water. For Jason, that truly was a game changer because, in the years to come, he would spend hours and hours playing in the water. It had become the place where he is most comfortable and actually able to interact with other kids.

Chapter 8

Life in a small town

Life in South Texas was good and we enjoyed adjusting to life in a small town. Our little town of Laguna Vista has a population of around 3,000 people and only one traffic light. I can't tell you how exciting it was, when a few years after moving here, we finally got a gas station. No more having to drive 8 miles into the town of Port Isabel to get gas. Not only that, we now had a close by place to get breakfast tacos in the morning.

One thing that took adjusting to was not having any family or friends close by. I was fortunate enough to make some nice friends who lived on my street and the realtor Janet, who helped us find our rental house, invited me to my very first SPINs meeting. SPINS stood for South Padre Island Neighbors and it was a group of women from the neighborhood who met once a month for lunch. In the years to come, Janet's friendship would be very valuable to me in terms of my family and also helping me with some of the projects that I would later become involved in.

For the first time in years, life seemed a little easier. Jason seemed happier and was very slowly starting to utter more words. He still had to be watched closely because he was faster than ever. He also was not the easiest to take to a restaurant or store. Occasionally, when we would have family come visit, we would venture out to a local restaurant and almost always leave there exhausted from the experience. Jason had a very difficult time sitting still and for being mostly nonspeaking, he sure could make a lot of noise.

As I made friends, we would be invited to birthday parties and I would bring both of our boys. Poor Dylan often spent a lot of his time having to help keep track of his brother. In no time at all Jason could get into something he wasn't supposed to, including one time when we thought his brother was watching him, but instead Jason had found his way into a bathroom and started painting nail polish on our friend's bathroom counter. We found it was usually easier to have friends come to our house because at least we could enjoy visiting a little more without having to constantly keep Jason from getting into things.

We tried our best to balance things so that Dylan could also enjoy his childhood. It was not easy because having Jason with us was more like having a two-year old along, only he was taller and much faster. He also could figure out how to escape or dismantle things much quicker that other kids his age. As we settled into our new community, Dylan became involved in band. Because he had been able to start band the year before we left the Northwest, he was already more advanced than his fellow classmates. He seemed to have a natural talent with the trumpet and ended up playing in the band his entire time in middle and high school. For us, it was nice to be able to come and watch him perform at times. I still have some of the video recordings of him performing, and almost always you could hear Jason making some type of noise in the background.

Shortly after we had moved to the area, we started looking to buy a home. We really needed a home in a court to help give Jason as safe of an environment as possible, since he would still walk in the street without ever looking for cars. There wasn't anything on the market that would work for us, so we decided to build a new house instead that would be in a quiet court. Actually, ours would be the very first house in that court, which was fine with us because it meant very little street traffic. I wish I could say everything went as planned and that few months later we moved into our house. The reality was though that the process took much longer than promised and as we kept paying thousands of dollars out of pocket for upgrades. That house was taking forever to get done. Meanwhile, we were still living in our 1200 square foot house that would become even tighter quarters every time my parents would come down to visit.

By the second summer we were in Texas, our builder promised us that our house would be ready to move in by the end of July. I decided to take my boys on a road trip back to Washington state, to have an extended trip to visit family and friends. My husband stayed behind to work and keep any eye on the house that we were building. The plan was that, by the time we would come back to Texas, the house should be ready to move in. I've come to learn that in life, you can make all the plans you want, but sometimes God has a different plan. While I was on my long road trip back to South Texas with my boys and nephew Christian in tow, Hurricane Dolly decided to make a direct path to South Padre Island and my new home town.

To make a long story short, the house we were building sustained enough damage that we had to start from scratch with a new builder and a new house on a new street. It was a devastating time for us. All of the money we had paid out in upgrades was gone too, because we had picked a builder who in the end was also a liar and a thief. So many people around us had sustained so much damage to their homes though, that at the end of the day, we were very fortunate because our rental house survived the storm unscathed. It was a pretty shocking drive back to our town to see all the damage and devastation that Hurricane Dolly caused. My poor nephew definitely picked a less than ideal time to visit. Add to the destruction the masses of mosquitos that hatched from all the standing water, and we definitely got to experience first-hand how strong a hurricane could be.

I mention this story because it really was an important part of our journey. Through the years going through everything that we had gone through with Jason only made us stronger in the end. Although the summer of dealing with the after effects of the hurricane was tough; we definitely were strong enough to survive this much unexpected event. We loved the area so much that we decided, even with the occasional threat of hurricanes, we would stay.

We now had to plan for a smaller budget for the next house and hoped and prayed that the next builder we chose would deliver as promised. I'm happy to say that as awful as the first building experience was, the next one with our builder, Bubba, went great. I could write an entire chapter about the housing experience, but this story is not about that. It is important to mention though, because so many kids with autism rely on having routine in their life. When it came to homes, our life was far from routine. Jason would actually move several more times in the years to come for various reasons. The house we are currently in is Jason's 10th house, and we have lived in it for over 3 years. This is definitely the longest time we have ever stayed in one place. Jason has become so accustomed to moving that every time we check out new houses under construction, he asks if it will be our new house.

Chapter 9

Settling into our new normal

For a couple years, we were settled into an easy routine. We spent most of our free time either at the pool, the beach or Schlitterbahn. South Texas gets very hot during the summer months, so being in the water was the easiest way to enjoy our time, and Jason loved playing in the water and at the beach. He had come a long way from that first year when he was scared of the water and wouldn't walk on the sand. Dylan made some nice friends, who Jason seemed to also like, so life was good. Something was about to happen though, that would make life even better.

My parents had originally moved to Washington state to be near us, and when we broke the news to them that we would be moving to Texas, they were very adamant that they would NEVER move to Texas. We understood that when we moved, but we also knew that they would visit. It was on their third visit with us that they told us that they had decided to move to our area. After a couple years of being on our own, we finally would have family close by again to help. We were so excited!

My mom and dad drove to Texas, bringing their cat and their parrot. While my mom stayed to help me with the boys, my husband and dad flew back to Washington to drive the moving trucks to South Texas. Little did we know how quickly things would change. Before those moving trucks were even halfway across the country, Jason would be in the hospital with a deadly infection.

I had mentioned before that Jason was unstable at times because of his toe walking. It was pretty common for Jason to have skinned up knees because he occasionally would fall. One night, my normally very active boy did not seem like himself. Because of his lack of verbal skills, he couldn't tell me what was wrong. I took his temperature and he did not have a fever, but I was concerned enough to have him sleep with me in my bed because I wanted to keep an eye on him. That next morning, he seemed ok and he still did not have a fever, so I went ahead and sent him to school. When he came home on the bus that afternoon, the bus driver called me over to the bus and told me that I needed to carry Jason off of the bus because he was having problems walking. I went to get him and noticed his knee was swollen and red.

That morning before school, I had noticed that Jason had a few of what looked like mosquito or bug bites on his legs. Those little red bumps now had a little puss point at the top of them. Of all nights, I had scheduled to host a Southern Living Party at my house that evening since my husband was out of town. I left my mom behind to prep the food for me and told her I would be back as soon as possible. Jason and I headed to the walk-in clinic in the next town over, to find out what was going on. After a quick examination, the nurse practitioner thought that he had some type of infection near his knee. She gave him an antibiotic shot right away and prescribed antibiotics for him to start taking immediately. She told me that it might take a little while to improve, but if the antibiotics were working, it shouldn't get any worse. She wanted to see him again in 24 hours if he seemed any worse.

We picked up our antibiotics and rushed home to a house full of people who had come for my party. I was so thankful to have my mom there to help. I put Jason to rest in his room with an ice pack for his knee and had Dylan help watch him while we did the party downstairs. I occasionally would run up to check on Jason, but he seemed ok.

The next morning, I kept him home and he still wasn't better. I had also noticed that he had a few more bumps that looked like bug bites and they had spread to his arms. By about midmorning, his knee started to swell a lot more and I became alarmed. I immediately took him back to the clinic, and the nurse took one look at him and told me to take him directly to the hospital. They were expecting us, so when we arrived at the emergency room, we were taken in to be seen by a doctor right away.

We had never seen this doctor before, but I sure recognized the type. He was one of those doctors who didn't want to take the time to really listen to what I was telling him. Jason was completely lethargic by this point and unable to walk. The doctor wanted to prescribe a different antibiotic and send him back home to see if it worked. Given the fact that we lived 45 minutes away from the hospital, and I was seeing my son completely fade in front of my eyes, I told the doctor that there was no way I was taking the chance to take him home because I was extremely concerned for my son. I had been through enough over the years with doctors who had failed my son and I would not back down. The doctor begrudgingly signed papers to have Jason admitted to the hospital with an attitude that felt like "ok lady, have it your way!".

Jason was 9 years old when this happened. It had taken me 9 years to finally trust my internal instinct and demand a certain treatment for my child. I truly was an expert when it came to my son, and I would no longer go against my better judgement to let a doctor risk my son's life or health. It turns out my instinct was correct because after 3 days in the hospital, the tests came back positive for a MRSA infection. If you aren't familiar with MRSA, it is deadly and initially can only be treated with an antibiotic that is given by IV. Once they can determine the type of infection, they then can figure out an antibiotic that can be given orally at home.

While in the hospital, a surgeon had to cut open the swollen skin on Jason's knee to drain the puss from the infection. The infection was very close to the bone and, if it had gone on much longer, the surgeon told me he could have lost his lower leg. How's that for mother's instinct?!

My husband and father were both driving across the country while all this was going on and I was never allowed to leave Jason alone in his hospital room. My mom was brand new to the area and did not know her way around at all. She was able to come out once, to stay with Jason, while I left the hospital for a couple hours. I remember going to a local clothing store to just walk around and do something other than sit day after day in a hospital room.

Our 5 day stay at the hospital was pretty traumatic for Jason. I knew trying to put an IV in his arm would be close to impossible, and I was correct. It took a team of 5 people to hold him still enough to get the IV in and then they taped it down as much as possible to keep it from popping out. Despite their best efforts and my best efforts to keep Jason still, there were several times that he moved too much and the IV had to be redone. The good news of this very tough experience is that Jason now can actually tolerate needles, when he needs bloodwork done. I think he learned the hard way that it's easier to sit still and let it happen versus having 5 people hold him down to do it.

To this day, Jason still gets distressed when it comes to cuts on his knees. Almost every time he has a doctor visit, the first thing he wants to show them is his knees, even if there are no cuts or scrapes. It makes me sad to think that almost nine years later, he still has such a clear memory of that experience. As scary as that experience was, there would be a much scarier one a few years down the road that would require a call to 911 and an ambulance. At least for the time being, everything was stable again, well, as stable as life could be when you are dealing with autism.

Chapter 10

A new addition to the family

The first many years of Jason's life, everything seemed to revolve around first finding out what was going on with Jason and then trying to "fix" Jason. There really wasn't much time to think of much else because Jason's condition definitely was a huge focus of our life. Dylan was such an awesome kid and we wanted to give him a sibling or two. After Jason was born, though, it became very clear that our hands were full and the idea of having any additional children definitely did not seem like a good idea. We knew Jason required a lot of attention, and the fact that we didn't yet understand what had caused all his issues, definitely caused us to be concerned that the same thing could happen to any additional children. We knew we could handle one special needs child, but we really didn't feel prepared to take the chance of having another one.

After a few years in Texas, though, I started talking to my husband about the possibility of adopting. I had a friend in town who recently had adopted two brothers from the foster care system and she told me all about the process. One of the selling points for me to my husband is that there was almost no cost involved in the process. It was more a matter of attending several classes to become approved by the state to do foster to adopt.

My husband has a tough work schedule which requires him to leave home very early in the morning. Getting him to classes that would be in the evening was definitely a sacrifice on his part, but amazingly enough, he agreed to go through the process with me.

The process took time and to make another long story short, we welcomed our beautiful daughter into our family in the Spring of 2011. Jason was in fifth grade and Dylan was a sophomore in high school. Our new daughter, Kimberly was just finishing up her freshman year of high school. I think people who didn't know us that well yet were a little confused when they found out this beautiful petite girl was our daughter. Kimberly is Hispanic, and has dark hair, skin and eyes. She definitely didn't look like us, but she fit right in with our family, so much so that in no time at all, she and Dylan would argue like they had been siblings for years. It was actually nice for Dylan to have a sibling who he could talk to that could answer back. They didn't always get along, but I don't know any siblings that close in age that don't have issues at times. It's nice to see that all these years later, as young adults, they have a connection and friendship. They actually like to hang out together whenever they get the chance.

I had my boys already and part of me always wanted a daughter. I had lived through years of what felt like a baby stage with Jason, so I definitely did not feel the need to adopt a young child. When we met Kimberly, she just seemed like she would be a great fit for our family. My husband wasn't so sure about adopting a teenager, but in no time at all, he saw what I saw and we were excited to add another child to our family.

There is a lot more to the adoption story, but the focus of this journey is Jason, so I don't want to stray too far off course. Kimberly is an important part of our journey though, so I thought it was important to mention how we came to be parents of three kids, when we only had two for many years.

In terms of Jason, having another sibling around was definitely a plus in so many ways. The more people Jason had to engage with, the more progress he would make. Kimberly had been around other kids with autism before, and she definitely had a great connection with Jason.

Kimberly joined our family right at the time that our school district was organizing their very first autism awareness walk. Our Special Services Director invited other parents to help plan and organize the event. I had never been part of anything like that before, but I was happy to help. That first year, one of my main jobs was to have a banner made. Talk about being out of my comfort zone! I knew absolutely nothing about banners or where to go to get one made. I was pretty proud of myself for finding a local business that made them and actually completing my main task. I helped a little with some other things that first year, but we had a parent volunteer who had experience with organizing walks, and she took care of most of the important details. Little did I know at the time that the next year I would be taking over pretty much everything she had done the first year and more. God was definitely preparing me for a bigger purpose, I just didn't realize it yet.

There was another very significant event that was happening in our lives right after the time that we were going through the adoption process. About 6 months after Kimberly joined our family, my father would find out he had adrenal cancer. It was extremely serious and he spent a long time in the same hospital that Jason had been at, before deciding to go to MD Anderson hospital in Houston. My father's type of cancer was pretty rare and almost always deadly, but thanks to his amazing doctors and a lot of prayer, he is a cancer survivor. If that wasn't hard enough to go through, my mom shortly thereafter was diagnosed with stage 3 breast cancer. She had to go through 6 months of chemo before having a mastectomy.

I like to mention these other big events that were happening in our life, because I think it's important for people to realize that as tough as things can be dealing with a child with autism, life still continues to happen. My parents moved to Texas to help us, but for around a year, we were able to be there to help them. I'm not sure things would have turned out so well for them had they stayed in the Northwest. I know I wouldn't have been able to help them the way I could with them living close by. It truly is amazing to look back on things years later and see how their desire to move here to help Jason may have actually played a part in helping them both survive cancer.

Chapter 11

More medical issues
to deal with

To be honest, the timeline of some of the things that I'm going to write about get a little fuzzy. I'll ask for forgiveness ahead of time if I get the sequence of events a little out of order. I did not keep a diary and although I have binders and binders of medical records, they are also not in chronological order and I'm hoping to finish writing this story in the next month instead of next year.

One issue that Jason had that needed to be addressed, was that Jason's orthopedic issues were getting worse again. It was wonderful when we lived within driving distance to Shriners Hospital, but here in the Valley, as our area of Texas is referred to, there were not many choices of doctors to see who could help him. Jason was referred to an orthopedic specialist outside of Houston, six hours away. After consulting with him, the determination was made that Jason was a good candidate for SPML surgery. (SPML stands for selective percutaneous myofascial lengthening.)

After the surgery, Jason would need time to recover and he would need to wear casts on both his legs for a month. We decided to do the surgery during Christmas vacation, so a few days after Christmas, my mom, Dylan, Jason and I all drove up to the Houston area. The surgery would require that we stay in the Houston area for a few days for a follow up visit. We were fortunate enough to have friends who lived close by who opened up their home to us.

The night before the surgery, Jason was busy inspecting the house we were staying in. In many rooms of the house, the lights were on timers and our friends were surprised to find many of their lights turning on in the middle of the night. Apparently, Jason reset their timers when we weren't watching him.

The surgery went as planned and after Jason was not able to walk at all. It was hard to see him in so much pain. We had a wheelchair to get him out to my car after the surgery, but after that, I had to carry him. My little boy was no longer that little, but luckily, I was able to handle him. I was definitely thankful that we didn't wait another year to do the surgery, because, by that time, he would have been too heavy for me to lift and we would have needed to rent a larger vehicle and travel with a wheelchair.

Within a couple of days, we had to force Jason to start walking with his casts on. It was difficult and painful for him, but it was necessary for the surgery to be successful. It really reminded me of how incredibly thankful I was that Jason was normally able to walk. Had we not been referred to the craniosacral therapist years earlier, there would have been the definite possibility that Jason may have not been able to walk. We have many friends who do have children who use wheelchairs and it definitely makes life a lot more complicated.

Fortunately for us, Jason's surgery was a complete success, and a month after surgery, his casts were removed and he walked better than he ever had. After that, he was fitted for new AFO's (ankle-foot orthosis) to help keep his heel-cords stretched. One thing that I found interesting at the time, was that this surgery was normally performed on kids with Cerebral Palsy. The only official diagnosis Jason ever had was Autism and, even though my earlier research regarding Jason's elevated bilirubin levels definitely pointed to kernicterus, which caused Cerebral Palsy, no doctor had ever mentioned CP to me in regards to Jason. I always figured that all of his issues were related to his autism diagnosis.

After a few months, it was time for an annual meeting with the school to go over Jason's educational plan. Jason had a very difficult time learning and retaining what he learned and he was still in a class for special needs students with a one on one aid. As a parent, it's hard to see your child struggle to learn. Even in 5th grade, Jason still struggled to read the most basic of words. It didn't help that he was so easily distracted.

It was during this meeting that the school psychologist made the suggestion of medicating Jason with a low dose patch called Daytrana, (methylphenidate) to help him to better focus and hopefully learn. Up until this point, Jason had never taken medication, and I was concerned because I knew he had adverse reactions to vaccines in the past, so I was afraid he may have issues with this patch. During that meeting, I was told that many other students had success with this patch and because it was such a low dose, it was considered very safe. I was given the name of a doctor that they recommended that a lot of their students used, and I made an appointment to learn more.

We met with the pediatrician and he seemed very knowledgeable. He treated several patients who had special needs. Up until this point, we had already tried two other pediatricians in the valley. I always would try to get one of the first appointments of the day and also let the staff know that Jason had autism and that it was very difficult for him to have long waits. I remember the first pediatrician had us wait in the exam room for two hours before he finally showed up. Two hours in any small space with Jason was a recipe for disaster. By the time this doctor came in, Jason was not in a good state. To top it off, after about 2 minutes, the doctor's cell phone rang and he excused himself while he stepped out of the room to take this "very important" call. When he strolled back in about 5 minutes later, he apologized for the delay and explained that it was an old college classmate that he hadn't spoken to in a long time. I was about ready to scream at this point, but Jason was agitated enough, so I kept my cool. The doctor then tried to examine Jason for all of about 2 minutes and Jason was not cooperative. This doctor then had the nerve to tell me that kids like my son often are difficult to examine. I then let him politely know that usually Jason was not a difficult patient, but he had waited two hours and that was more the issue than anything else. Needless to say, we NEVER made a follow up visit with this doctor.

The next doctor we tried was much better, but after the initial visit, we never saw him again. Even though I would schedule an appointment with him, we were always seen by his much younger and less experience colleague that I was not very impressed with. After these first two experiences, we gave up on pediatricians for a while and just used the local walk in clinic if we needed any medical attention. This new pediatrician seemed worthwhile.

One thing I liked about this new pediatrician is that he really seemed to take his time to get to know about Jason and his medical history. He assured me that this Daytrana patch was definitely something very safe that may be helpful for Jason. I decided we should give it a try, especially since he would only wear the patch during school hours, so basically about 8 hours a day. I wanted Jason to be able to focus more, so he had a better chance of learning. I felt it was worth giving it a try.

I put the patch on Jason that first morning, just before the bus came, and then sent him off to school. An hour later, my phone rang and it was the school nurse calling to let me know that Jason was in her office, and he had been throwing up. He had been completely fine before leaving for school, so my first thought was that he was having a reaction to the patch. I picked him up and brought him home. I called his doctor to let them know I thought he might be having a reaction to this new medication. His doctor told me he thought it was just a coincidence, and he didn't think his throwing up was related to the patch. I was so busy taking care of my sick son, that I took the doctors word for it and kept using the patch for Jason. Looking back at it now, I only wish I would have done a simple internet search for side effects from Daytrana, but unfortunately once again, I had blindly trusted our doctor who definitely had more knowledge about this patch than I did.

The next day, Jason seemed to be feeling better so I sent him back to school, thinking maybe it was just a 24-hour bug. Keep in mind though, Jason would rarely get more than a common cold, so he being sick was definitely out of the norm for him.

One week later, I received another call from school informing me that Jason was vomiting again. At that point I was thinking that whatever he had the week before must still somehow be lingering. I had no reason to consider the Daytrana patch was to blame because Jason's doctor assured me that wasn't the case.

Three weeks after Jason started using Daytrana, the doctor raised the dosage. It is normal to start them on the lowest dose and gradually increase the dosage. To be honest, I was getting good reports from school that he was calmer in the classroom and able to sit longer periods of time and focus on his work. It appeared that the patch was doing its job.

Four weeks from the time we started the patch, which was one week after the dose was raised, Jason was once again throwing up in the morning. This time he started before he even went to school, so I just kept him home. I honestly did not know what was going on with him, but he wasn't running a fever, so I just let him rest in his favorite recliner that was in the front room of our house. He spent most of the day just sleeping in the recliner. He's was normally a very active kid, so it was very clear that he wasn't feeling well.

Dylan and Kimberly came home after school that day and Jason was still resting in the recliner in the front room. A little while after the kids got home from school, Dylan walked by the room where Jason had been sleeping on the recliner. I still remember Dylan's words. He called out to me and said "mom, there's something wrong with Jason". I immediately came from the next room to see what was going on. Jason's lifeless body was hanging off the side of the recliner. Thankfully Dylan had been trained as a lifeguard, and his training kicked in immediately. He helped move Jason to the rug on the floor and place him on his side. Jason's eyes were rolled back in his head and he was foaming at the mouth. Even worse than that was he was completely unresponsive.

These next few minutes were some of the worst moments that I have ever experienced as a mother. I am so thankful that I had both my older kids there at the time because I had lost my ability to function other than to keep crying out to Jason to try to bring him back. Dylan got on the phone and called 911 and Kimberly was doing her best to help me. I can't begin to estimate how long it took for the ambulance to arrive, but at the time, it seemed to take too long. Dylan had to place a second call to 911 to find out why the ambulance wasn't there, and the operator told them that they had arrived, but nobody was home. The ambulance had gone to the wrong location! In our neighborhood, there was a street and a court that shared the same name. Instead of coming to our court, they made a mistake and went to the house on the street.

Jason was completely unresponsive until maybe two to three minutes before the ambulance arrived. That moment when his eyes returned to normal and he could actually see me again is a moment I will never forget. Although he did have a heartbeat during this episode, he truly appeared to no longer be with us. It was determined that Jason had a grand mal seizure, and he was rushed off to the hospital. His dad had been out kiteboarding during all of this and he did not find out about it until we were already in the ambulance about to head to the hospital.

Jason was given seizure meds in the ambulance to help prevent him from having another episode. I had no experience with seizures, but by this point I was pretty convinced that it was brought on by the Daytrana patch. Once Jason was examined at the hospital and declared stable, he was released to go home with us. We were to follow up with his pediatrician and a neurologist to determine what brought this seizure on.

To save you all the long not so exciting details of those follow up doctor visits, I will give you the summary. Even though I was 99% sure that Jason's seizure was caused by the patch he was using, the doctor informed me that about 30% of kids with autism have seizure disorders (epilepsy).They often start having seizures when they are reaching puberty, if they didn't already have them when they were younger. Keep in mind again, I am "just a mom" only knowing what I have experienced with my own kids. I did not have years of medical school or years of medical practice to fall back on.

I had the option to not put him on seizure medicine and wait and see if he would have another seizure or not, but that option did come with its own set of risks. If I was wrong and his seizure was not a side effect of the patch, then any additional seizures he may have could make the epilepsy more difficult to control. In addition to that, by this time we had moved again, and our latest house also had a pool and Jason spent a lot of time playing in it. If he had a seizure in the pool and we weren't watching him at that moment, he could easily drown.

Having the memory of my lifeless son on the floor still fresh in my mind, I knew I needed to err on the side of caution, so I put him on the seizure medication. Needless to say, I would never put him on medication again for ADHD. I couldn't take the chance of being wrong and losing my son. The safest thing to do was to start the seizure meds. The doctor told me he would need to be 3 years seizure free before we could consider stopping this new medication.

Skipping ahead three years down the road, Jason never had another seizure. My initial instinct that the Daytrana patch was to blame was spot on. What I still to this day do not understand is, how his pediatrician, who seemed to be very familiar with this drug did not take the time to read the side effects available with the package insert. Vomiting was a very common side effect and **seizures** were also listed as a rare side effect. As in many cases when it came to Jason's health, he seemed to have more severe reactions than most other kids when it came to vaccines and now some drugs. It was really becoming disheartening as a parent to once again be failed by a doctor that I put my trust in. To know that I could have lost my son that day, when I had already reached out to his doctor, only to have my previous concerns dismissed. This truly angered me! Time after time, the medical profession has not only failed to help my son, but has been responsible for causing him more harm.

I wish I had done more research ahead of time, but, honestly, that is what I expected my doctor to do. With the added fact that the school psychologist also was recommending this; I just made the mistake of trusting the wrong people with my son. It has taken me years to get there, but I now trust myself much more than any other doctor or "specialist" when it comes to the health of my son.

Just for reference when searching on the internet, this is what I found when it came to information on Daytrana.

Daytrana side effects

Get emergency medical help if you have signs of an allergic reaction to Daytrana: hives; difficulty breathing; swelling of your face, lips, tongue, or throat.

Stop using Daytrana and call your doctor at once if you have:

- redness, swelling, blistering, or skin color changes where the skin patch was worn (may also spread to other areas);
- a seizure;
- chest pain, trouble breathing, feeling like you might pass out;
- changes in your vision;
- hallucinations (seeing or hearing things that are not real), new behavior problems, aggression, hostility, paranoia; or
- numbness, pain, cold feeling, unexplained wounds, or skin color changes (pale, red, or blue appearance) in your fingers or toes.

Methylphenidate can affect growth in children. Tell your doctor if your child is not growing at a normal rate while using this medicine.

Common Daytrana side effects may include:

- dizziness, mood swings;
- tics;
- nausea, vomiting, stomach pain, loss of appetite, weight loss;
- sleep problems (insomnia); or
- skin redness, bumps, or itching where a patch was worn.

This is not a complete list of side effects and others may occur. Call your doctor for medical advice about side effects. You may report side effects to FDA at 1-800-FDA-1088.

Source for this is
(https://www.drugs.com/daytrana.html)

One other side note was information that I learned later on from my own daughter Kimberly about this drug. When Kim was still living in foster care, she was also given a patch to wear for ADHD. She told me that it always made her feel dizzy and nauseous, so much so that she hardly would eat all day to avoid having her stomach hurt. Luckily for her, she had a great foster mom at the time that paid attention to what was going on and was able to get the doctors to take her off of the patch. It truly is sad how easily these patches are prescribed. My daughter does not have ADHD, but in the foster care system it has become the norm to medicate so many of the kids.

As for Jason, I can only imagine how he was feeling while using this patch. He does not have the verbal skills to tell us if he is dizzy or nauseated. It had to get to the point of almost losing him, before we realized how dangerous this particular drug could be.

Chapter 12

Helping Jason find his voice

In early 2015, I read an article that really caught my interest. It was about someone who made the decision to go 24 hours without speaking, to better understand autism. When I read about it, I thought to myself that is something that I should try. As a parent, we all try to do what we can to help our kids, but often I think it can be very difficult to really understand what they are going through. Since Jason lives every day of his life having very limited speaking skills, I wanted to get an idea of what life was like for Jason. I made the decision to not only not speak for 24 hours, but also not to write, type, or text, because Jason also doesn't have the ability to communicate in writing either.

At the time I decided to do this, Jason's older brother was going through basic training with the Air Force. I had really been missing him, but every few weeks during his training, we were able to receive a short phone call from him. We had just received a call a couple days before this challenge, so I thought the timing to go nonverbal was as good as it was going to get.

I actually made a video with me—and Jason in it—explaining what I was about to do and why. Once I posted the video on my Facebook page that was the start of my 24-hour challenge. Going 24 hours without communicating, using speech, or writing, would definitely prove to be a challenge. It would have been easier to just plan on staying home instead of navigating regular life without speaking. I wanted to really get the full experience though, so I planned on going out in public during my 24 hours, and when I did, I also wore a handwritten sign on my shirt explaining that I was going nonverbal for 24 hours to better understand autism.

If you think I may have felt a little uncomfortable going around like this, you would be correct. The way I looked at it though, was that my son and thousands of others like him don't get to choose if they are comfortable or not. Every moment of their life they have to deal with the reality of their disability, so I proudly took on the challenge to show my son and others like him my support. I also hoped to get a better insight into what their life feels like for them.

I let my husband Scott know of my plans ahead of time. I don't think he had an opinion about it one way or another. What I didn't realize until I started, was how much more difficult he would make the challenge for me.

Within the first 10 minutes of the challenge, I realized that my husband didn't want to try to communicate with me since I wasn't able to answer back. Keep in mind, I could still hear and I could also nod my head or try to gesture with my hands, but Scott just decided it was easier to not even really talk to me and just go on with whatever he was planning on doing that day. Just minutes into my challenge, I literally found myself already slamming the dryer door a little harder out of frustration. It was at that moment that I got my first taste of how difficult this challenge would be.

A little while into the challenge, I came into the backyard and found my husband cutting down my absolute favorite grapefruit tree. I tried gesturing away that I wanted him to stop, but since I wasn't able to speak, he basically ignored me and kept cutting.

Two hours into the challenge, my cell phone rang. I saw the number was a San Antonio number, and right away I had a feeling it could be Dylan calling from Basic Training. Any parent that has ever had a child leave home for the military will understand how completely devastating it can be to miss a call from your child when they are going through basic training or boot camp. I wasn't expecting Dylan to be able to call for at least another week, but here I was looking at my phone ringing. I missed my son and wanted to do anything possible not to miss his call. I also knew he was missing us and I didn't want to disappoint him by not answering. I also was so committed to supporting Jason by doing this challenge, and I knew I couldn't let him down.

I did the only thing I could think of and that was to answer the phone, but not talk. Instead I made strange noises so Dylan knew I was there and I ran the phone out to Scott, who was still massacring my beloved grapefruit tree. I handed him the phone, and I still remember his words to Dylan. He didn't take the time to explain why I couldn't talk to him, he only said I was "doing some autism thing". I truly wanted to scream out of frustration, because I at least hoped he would explain what I was doing, so Dylan would understand why I couldn't talk to him. Of my entire experience over the 24 hours of going nonverbal, this moment by far was the most heartbreaking for me. I just wanted to breakdown and cry at the moment because I missed Dylan so much at this point, and here I wasn't able to speak to him. That moment definitely was an eye opener for me of how extremely difficult this challenge would be.

The rest of the day didn't get any easier. I remember napping off and on for a while because I felt so isolated not being able to speak. The one interesting thing was, Jason seemed to absolutely love the fact that I wasn't speaking and that I could only gesture. He purposely took advantage of the situation by doing things he knew I didn't allow, but I wasn't able to verbally tell him not to do them. He clearly understood my gestures, but laughed and ignored me as if it was a game.

The next morning, we went to church as a family. I wore my sign and people read it and didn't really say too much. I did start noticing that the few people that did speak to me were speaking louder and slower than normal, as if my inability to speak somehow also made me hard of hearing. After church, we stopped at Walmart and I ran into a few friends who knew what I was doing, because they had seen the Facebook video.

My one saving grace during the morning was my daughter Kimberly. She was the only one who actually spoke to me and would take the time to try to understand my gestures. She was able to decipher what I wanted. She even texted on my behalf to a friend of mine, who was in town for the day, who wanted to hang out. I ended up going with my friend and Jason to the Farmer's Market on the island. If I thought Jason was tough at home with me not speaking, I soon found out that having him in public was much more challenging. Luckily, my friend Velma was there to help keep him from running off, and we made our way through the market.

We ran into my friend Cristina there, who also knew about the challenge. She suddenly seemed to use her hands more when she was speaking to me, as if I might not understand her words. It really was an interesting experience to see how people I knew actually changed how they communicated with me, just because I wasn't speaking. I think the greatest insight into my experience was, how many people chose to just ignore me, because trying to communicate with me was too difficult for them.

I found during my 24 hours of this challenge, that what I craved the most was human interaction. It didn't take long to feel isolated, when I wasn't able to easily communicate. My friend Velma is normally a very chatty person, and I often am on the listening end of many of our conversations. During our time together though, she was so much quieter than normal. She would try to tell me something, but because she couldn't understand my gestures when I was trying to respond, she instead became quiet herself. I remember thinking the entire time when I was with her of what I wanted to tell her once I could speak again. It became a little overwhelming, because, there was so much I wanted to say, but couldn't.

Knowing that entire time how much I wanted to say and having to hold it in, made me realize that I'm sure my son also had a lot to say, but never would be able to tell me. It really made me sad to think of how much I missed out of his daily life, because he couldn't tell me about it. It's easy to understand why he would be content not interacting with people, because over a lifetime, it probably just became easier to not try.

Those 24 hours were the longest 24 hours I think I had ever experienced. I couldn't wait for the time to be over and be able to speak again. I gained such insight during those hours on how incredibly difficult it was to be nonspeaking in this very verbal world of ours. I especially realized how isolating it was, and for me, it really helped me to realize how important human interaction is for everyone.

Think of someone who is in a wheelchair who doesn't have the ability to communicate. I think for the most part, people pretty much don't even take the time to acknowledge them. After this challenge I understand just a small aspect of what their life may feel like, and I go out of my way to find ways to interact with anyone who is nonspeaking, especially someone in a wheelchair. It actually is such a treat to connect with them at their level and to see their eyes light up when they realize that they are no longer treated as if they are invisible.

My 24-hour challenge left such an impact on my life. I was able to better understand why meltdowns happen for my son. I was also able to understand why he often just is in his own little world. Without a way to communicate, it becomes easier to become isolated. I finished the challenge more determined to find a way to know my son better. I even set up a special

Facebook page just for him so that people could get to know more about him. Since he wasn't able to tell people about himself and what his life is like, I wanted share things about him so that people understand him better. Since starting the page, I think people actually feel like they know him at a level that they weren't able to before. I also encourage people to share with me pictures and their experiences when they see him, so I could know more about what his day was like.

My original video about my 24 -hour challenge was shared several thousand times on Facebook. I even set up a special Facebook page called "The 24-Hour Autism Challenge" to help spread awareness. I did my best to spread the message about what my time living without speaking or writing was like, and encouraged others to also take the challenge. I know many who tried, but only a couple who were able to endure the entire 24 hours. Most people gave up after only a few hours, which really proves the point of just how difficult it is to be nonspeaking in a world that speaks.

I was invited to speak at a high school about autism and I told the students about my experience of going 24 hours without speaking. They were so moved by what I told them, that one of the students decided to bring the challenge to her school as part of her senior project. At the end of the year, approximately 60 high school students did an 8-hour autism challenge. They did not speak the entire day at school and also gave up their cell phones. It really was incredible to see so many of them take the challenge to help them better understand autism.

I spread the word about the challenge the following year during the month of April, which is traditionally known as autism awareness month. I did modify the challenge to four or more hours because most people truly couldn't handle much more than that. Four hours is enough to get a taste of how it feels to be nonverbal, and that is the point I was hoping to get across. I have no idea how many people have taken the challenge, but I was really proud that our entire local police department signed up to do the challenge, as well as many people who attended our local autism walk. Little by little, hopefully people will take the time to understand autism better, because when they do, life gets a little better for everyone.

Photo Gallery

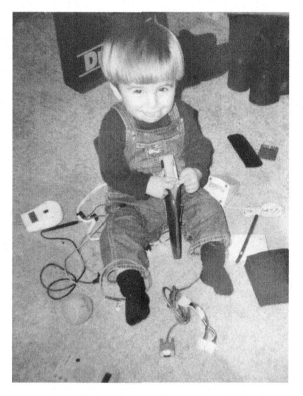

Jason's head grew faster than his body.
This was a very rare picture where Jason was
actually looking towards the camera.

Jason always had a full head of hair. Notice how he was looking away from the camera. Even to this day, we often have to take several pictures to get one where he is actually looking in the direction of the camera.

*Enjoying living near the beach after
so many years living in the Northwest.*

Jason has been in school with these same friends since first grade. They are affectionately known as the Fab Five.

Our beautiful family of five.

At Dylan's basic training graduation.

Jason with his Oma and Opa at church.

*Dylan's graduation. A few months later,
he would leave and Jason has missed
him ever since.*

Dogs are Jason's best friends. He's never met a dog he didn't love. He definitely will talk to them much more than he will talk to people.

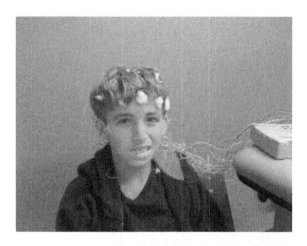

Jason enduring one of many medical tests.

One of Jason's doctors told us that he may never walk. Here is Jason proving him wrong.

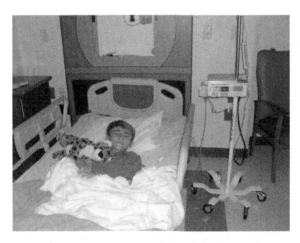

This was taken during the time where Jason was hospitalized for MRSA.

Jason wearing his AFOs. He went through many pairs of these over the years as he grew.

The boy who used to be terrified of the water, now loves it.

Jason with Mrs. Elsa Garcia who was the person who organized the first autism walks in our school district.

Jason with his Opa at one of his baseball games.

Love the relationship that our kids have!

*Jason at his very first prom that was held
at church in Brownsville Texas.*

Jason loves playing at the beach.

Jason still loves playing with toys. He can also create incredible mazes and drawings too.

Jason after he got ahold of the clippers.

Waiting to get tickets to the waterpark. This was the start of a three-year process to help Jason get comfortable going in the park after years of anxiety.

Pictures from Jason's senior prom and graduation.

Support from family has made such a difference in Jason's life. The picture above includes his aunt Michelle, Uncle Frank and cousins Daniel, Christian and Heidi.

Blessed to have such a supportive family!

Chapter 13

Autism

I have to say that it really is an interesting experience for me to sit down and write about so many events that have occurred over Jason's lifetime. As I read back what I've already written, I remember other things that I want to mention, so again, forgive me if some things are not always in order. For some reason, it was easiest to write about the first 5 years of Jason's life because during that time, I was obsessed with helping my son. To this day, I still want to help him to live his best life, but I have also learned to accept the fact that, short of a miracle or major medical breakthrough, autism will always be something that Jason will have to live with.

As difficult as that last sentence is to write, I am at peace about it at this point in our journey. The Serenity Prayer definitely helps with that. It is so simple, but yet for me it holds so much meaning. If you don't know it, it states- "God, grant me the serenity to accept the things I can't change, the courage to change the things I can, and the wisdom to know the difference." I may not mention God all that often in our story, but make no mistake, my faith in God is truly the foundation of my life.

At my deepest and darkest times of sorrow, I have always been able to give my worries and burdens to God and know that ultimately, He is control. I stopped worrying and started trusting that God truly has a plan. That doesn't mean that I haven't tried to bargain with God along the way and ask for a miracle healing, because I have. What I am at peace with is God's plan for Jason's life. I have already experienced so many wonderful things because of this journey, and I know because of it, I have also been able to help other people too. If Jason didn't have autism, I know that so much of what I do now in my life would have never happened and, honestly, I think my life would not be anywhere near as fulfilling and joyful as it is now, without all that we have gone through.

I do want to mention that along the way, there was no shortage of well-meaning friends or acquaintances who thought they had the next big cure to help my son. It's a difficult thing to have someone come to you with something that you know nothing about, but they have "testimonies" from other parents who have talked about how this product helped their child. I spent the money and tried several different products through the years to help Jason. Unfortunately, to this point, none of them have made much of a difference in helping him recover from the effects of autism.

There is so much that I will be talking about in the chapters to come, but before I continue, I want to talk about some of the elephants in the room so to speak. I have found that there are many trains of thought when it comes to autism, and I respect everyone's option to have their own take on how they look at autism. There are those out there who want to "celebrate" autism. In fact, some young adults with autism who have found their voice either through assisted technology devices or otherwise, have also had their own views when it comes to how autism affects them and how they want people to perceive them.

I have huge respect for people living with autism. They often deal with incredible hurdles, to be able to function in regular everyday environments. Through the years of being around so many people living with autism, I have truly enjoyed spending time with them and finding ways to connect with them and help them feel more connected to the world around them. Autism is referred to as a spectrum disorder because, though many have some similar characteristics, it affects people differently. There is a saying that goes "if you know one person with autism, you know one person with autism". Just like anyone else, each individual can be so different in how they are affected. Some people with autism can speak and are considered geniuses. Some who don't have verbal skills can also be brilliant. There are others though who definitely test on the lower IQ scale and then there are those whom an IQ test really cannot accurately assess how intelligent they are. My son, for example, still is very limited verbally, but he can build the most interesting mazes and structures out of blocks or dominoes. He is also completely obsessed with central vacuum systems for the home, so much so, that he has ordered component parts for them on Amazon, when he finds a device that is still signed in. He has also probably hundreds of times drawn out schematics of our house and where all the plugs-ins and pipes should be, if we ever install a central vacuum system. We have had two homes in years past with this system, and he absolutely loves plugging the hose into the wall and vacuuming. Unfortunately, he doesn't have the same fondness for vacuuming with our regular upright vacuum. I wish he would though because, we have a house with pets that constantly requires vacuuming.

When it comes to my personal opinion on autism, I can definitely say that I am not in the camp of "celebrating autism." Autism is fascinating in how it affects some people, but even more often, it is heartbreaking to see the anxiety and the struggle that come with living with autism. My son, has through the years, had self-injurious behavior and extreme anxiety. He is only considered moderate when it comes to autism; the ones on the severe side of the spectrum have it much worse, and so do their families. I cannot celebrate that, instead it breaks my heart to see what he and others have to go through every day.

I think a lot of us autism families put on a good front of mostly showing our kids in the best light possible. I personally tend to show Jason's best side, the fun and goofy kid he is. Sometimes I'll have to take 20 pictures of him before I get one of him that shows his beautiful smile. Most of the other pictures show him looking everywhere, except the camera and often with him putting his hand on his face or head. I don't show the meltdowns or times he is extremely distressed. I have done such a good job of showing that my son at his best that people are often shocked when they see him having a meltdown. For us, those meltdowns are fewer and farther between now, but they do still happen.

We have friends who have kids with autism, who sometimes are covered in cuts and bruises from their kids attacking them. I have one friend that suffered a serious injury from her son who choked her during a meltdown, and she was terrified to seek medical help, because she didn't want anything to happen to her child. The reality of autism isn't the picture of the cute little kid who likes watching the ceiling fan spin, it's unfortunately more realistic to see a child hitting himself or slamming his head into a wall. Autism hurts our kids and it hurts their families.

The fact that, to this day, Jason cannot say his name to the clarity that he could before he regressed after his vaccines at 15 months of age, is still a reminder of what he has lost because of autism. I will not ever celebrate the fact that he has autism. That is no different than someone who wouldn't celebrate the fact that someone has cancer. What I do celebrate though, is every achievement, no matter how small, that my son makes, despite living with autism. He truly has to work so hard to do things that come almost naturally to others. Just learning how to tie a shoe took around 15 years, despite every occupational therapist having that as a goal for him. In the end, after starting Jason on Camel's milk, he suddenly taught himself a new method of how to tie his shoes and it is one that now his therapists are using to teach other kids.

Please don't confuse my not being a fan of autism with anything less that total love for my incredible son. As much as I wish he didn't have to live with autism, I do see the blessings and gifts that have come of it as well. My son has the ability to make me laugh and see life from a whole new perspective. I love being his mom, and even though I didn't plan on having him live with me my entire life, I am prepared to take care of him as long as I can, or until we can find a great place for him where he would rather live.

When I see kids his age hanging out with friends, playing sports, getting a driver license, getting jobs, having girlfriends, going off to college or any of the millions of "normal" activities and milestones most kids get to experience in life, I have to be honest that my heart breaks that my son will for the most part will not get to do many of those things. I have become determined to give my son and others as many opportunities as possible to experience life, but even so, there will always be so many experiences, that because of his autism, he won't get to experience.

Jason has definitely come a long way through the years and is always making progress. He loves kids and playing at playgrounds. He gives big hugs and definitely appreciates seeing a pretty girl. He just turned 18 recently, and his main gift was a new Thomas Train tower that fits with the other multitude of train and track sets that he already has. As much as we want to transition him out of the toy stage, it is something that still brings him so much joy. He's six foot three inches tall, and honestly, he's just a giant child.

Don't get me wrong, I count my blessings all the time that he is happy and has no serious health issues. We have so many friends who have children who are medically fragile or so much more severe behaviorally. Our main goals for Jason early on were for him to walk and then get toilet trained. We accomplished both of those by age 5 and those accomplishments have given us a lot more options when it comes to Jason living more independently.

Our next major goal is to continue to help Jason speak and find his voice. His speech is definitely still a work in progress. I remember having a very vivid dream where I was having a normal conversation with Jason. I woke up in tears because it was so real and something I long for so much. I realize though, that those conversations may not ever happen here one earth, but have faith that one day in heaven I will be able to truly have those conversations with him that we couldn't have here on earth.

I have come to a point of acceptance that Jason will most likely have to deal with the effects of autism the rest of his life, but I have also become much more knowledgeable along the way. The more I study the subject, the more I feel led to share with others what I have learned. At this point in my life, it's safe to say I have probably spent thousands of hours reading books, medical studies, articles, and pretty much everything I can get my hands on when it comes to figuring out what is behind this incredible rise of autism.

Chapter 14

The "V" word

I had mentioned in the last chapter about speaking about some "elephants in the room". I am about to speak about what I think it the biggest elephant out there- vaccines. Before I broach this topic, I'd like to say that it definitely is much easier to remain silent when it comes to this subject. Unfortunately, I feel I have a moral obligation to talk about our personal experiences when it comes to Jason's reactions to the vaccines he was given. He is definitely not the "one in a million" statistic that is so commonly put out there. I have come to find out that when it comes to vaccines, it's like playing Russian Roulette with my child's health. For some, they can endure the vaccines with no immediate adverse reaction, for others, the effects can be very severe, including death. There is no shortage of personal stories of families who have lost their children due to a vaccine. Unfortunately, our society has become blind to the truth of the lives damaged or lost, and for some, they just consider our children collateral damage for the "greater good".

I still question to this day why Jason was given vaccines while his jaundice level was still so high. Vaccines should not be given to someone who is not well. Jason was not well and he was given vaccines anyway. When he was failing to thrive during his first 9 months of life, the vaccines continued and he continued to deteriorate. I was never fully informed of what serious side effects there were with vaccines. Looking back now, to how we almost lost Jason to the side effects of the Daytrana patch, it only makes sense that there is something different going on in his body, that causes him to have severe reactions, when other people don't.

Obviously, with the current rate of autism in boys being somewhere around 1 in every 26 boys, Jason isn't the only one with this issue. The regression that we experienced when he completely lost all speech for 3 years, was real and witnessed by many. At the time, we didn't know to put the pieces together to point towards the vaccines, but over time, looking back through his medical history, there is no doubt that vaccines played a large role in the autism that Jason lives with today.

I am not going to go into detail about everything I have learned about vaccines in this book, because it is truly a very complex subject. What I can say for myself is, even though at the time I had no clue that vaccines could even have serious side effects other than a mild fever, my own instinct kicked in to realize that every time

Jason received more vaccines, we lost him even more. For a while, also based on my own instincts, I thought it made more sense to at least space out the vaccines instead of giving them all at once. Unfortunately, even trying that at age 6 proved to also not work well for Jason, and I was advised by his doctor not to vaccinate him anymore.

In past few years, vaccines have become a very highly contested topic, and, because of that, my research has intensified. What I have learned has brought me to my knees. I have gone through times of blaming myself for not doing my own research ahead of time, but at the same time, that is what I expect of the doctors who treated my son. Unfortunately, I have learned much too late that doctors are not researchers and, for the most part, they blindly follow the vaccine schedule put out by the CDC.

Many doctors have also come to the realization that they have caused unintentional harm to hundreds if not thousands of their patients. Those doctors are speaking out; but the pharmaceutical industry is a multibillion-dollar industry and their money not only controls most of the media, but it also controls politicians. (Just think of how many commercials you see that are for pharmaceutical products.) The pharmaceutical companies also control a lot of the content you will find online which makes finding the truth regarding vaccines much more difficult to search for.

There are also some brave politicians that have also sounded the alarm when it comes to safety of vaccines, but, unfortunately, until the pharmaceutical industry is held liable for the damage their vaccines cause, the out of control vaccine schedule will most likely continue to grow. I have read that every vaccine can bring in 4 BILLION dollars. There is a lot of incentive to keep up the myth that vaccines are necessary and safe.

Back when I was a kid, we received vaccines for around 7 different diseases that were given in only three vaccinations. This is the list of the recommended vaccines for the 1970's:

Tetanus

Diphtheria

Pertussis (whooping cough)

Polio

Measles

Mumps

Rubella

Protection for the remaining seven diseases on the schedule, however, required only three vaccinations:

Polio vaccination

Combined vaccination for Tetanus, Diphtheria, and Pertussis (DTP vaccine)

Combined vaccination for Measles, Mumps, and Rubella (MMR vaccine).

As of early 2014, the U.S. immunization schedule for children ages 0-6 years includes recommendations for the following vaccinations:

Hepatitis B

Rotavirus

Diphtheria, Tetanus, and Pertussis (combined DTaP vaccine)

Hib (Haemophilus influenzae type b)

Pneumococcal

Polio (inactivated vaccine)

Influenza

Measles, Mumps, and Rubella (combined MMR vaccine)

Varicella (chickenpox)

Hepatitis A

Meningococcal (certain high-risk groups only)

In addition, the 7-18 years schedule recommends human papillomavirus (HPV) vaccination and meningococcal vaccination.

It's easy to see that there has been a huge increase in the number of vaccines that are given to kids now versus even when I was a child. Back then, in my entire lifetime, I had only met about 5 kids with disabilities. Kids, overall, were pretty healthy back then, despite the fact that most of us had chickenpox and often measles. My parents, who are now in their 80's, received even less vaccines and they lived through all the normal childhood illnesses. What's really sad and shocking at the same time is that none of the vaccines given today have ever been safety tested against placebos, and they also have not studied to see if the combination of them is safe to give together. In addition to that, it's obvious that more vaccines do not mean people are healthier. So many people I know have issues with asthma, eczema, autoimmune disease, epilepsy, and so many other conditions that we rarely saw years ago.

Most people do not know that back in the late 1980's the United States Congress passed legislation that removed liability from the pharmaceutical companies from any death or injury their vaccines may cause. Instead, there is something called VAERS, which is the Vaccine Adverse Event Reporting System. Every doctor is required to report vaccine adverse events (aka side effects.) Unfortunately, most doctors fail to report reactions, and it is estimated that only about 1% of all vaccine reactions are reported. Even with that, over 4 BILLION dollars has been paid out through the Vaccine Injury Court that is run by the government, to people who have suffered vaccine injuries or deaths.

What I can say for me after all my own research, is that Jason definitely had serious adverse reactions to his vaccines. Those side effects definitely played a part in his diagnosis of autism. I am truly thankful that I listened to my own intuition and stopped vaccinating him when I did. Had we continued with the vaccines, there would be a very high likelihood of him having epilepsy for life, as well as being even more severely affected by autism.

Often, when I meet a family who has a child with autism, the more severe cases of autism that I observe are among those individuals who continued to receive vaccines. I highly encourage people read anything they can on the subject if they want more information. Please don't believe the tagline put out by the pharmaceutical companies that the "science is settled," because that is one of the biggest lies of our times. I also encourage everyone to go check out the CDC website and read the ENTIRE vaccine insert for the vaccines they are considering on giving their children. Resources are provided at the end of this book.

Like I said, it truly is a very complicated subject and I can't say often enough, that every person who chooses to vaccinate, owes it to themselves and their children to be better informed before they ever step into the doctor's office. Read information on both sides of the subject. I had absolutely no idea what was in the vaccines that we had injected into our kids, and when I found out, I was shocked. If you understand the risks involved and still choose to vaccinate, at least you will be informed and can be better prepared to notice if they do suffer adverse reactions.

An author of a book I recently read, named Forrest Maready, had a good way of characterizing what it's like once you have become informed about vaccines. He compared it to when the American soldiers first stepped inside a concentration camp during World War II. Up until this point, everyone was told that the concentration camps were just factories. People believed that, because that was what they were told. Once they actually went inside and saw that they were not factories, but instead that people were being starved, tortured and burned alive, nothing anyone could tell them would ever make them believe that they were only factories.

I have the same conclusion when it comes to vaccines. I used to blindly believe that vaccines were beneficial because that was what I was told. After all, we have all been told that repeatedly on the news every time there is another measles outbreak, right? It wasn't until I personally did the research to learn more, that I learned that the subject was not that simple. Despite the possible good intentions that vaccines manufacturers started out with, at the end of the day the ingredients in vaccines are causing more harm than good.

We recently had a guest stay at our Airbnb that is behind our house. This guest was staying with us for a week and I got into a long conversation with him. He was asking a lot of questions in regards to Jason, and it turned out he was a retired cardiologist. Long story short, he was completely floored several times at how many doctors had failed Jason through the years. Not only that, this was a doctor who completely believed in vaccines and also thought anyone who didn't vaccinate should be put in the category of a crazy "antivaxxer". (Side note- the term antivaxxer couldn't be further from the truth for many of us, because we DID vaccinate. The correct label if you want to give one should be "exvaxxer") What this retired cardiologist learned from our conversations though, definitely raised some serious questions for him. So much so, that he even brought up the subject with his adult daughter in regards to his two beautiful granddaughters. Since he was with us for a week, I shared with him a book I had just finished called "The Autism Vaccine". I just wanted to get a little insight from his perspective of his impressions of what the book was about. I was happy to find that he didn't point out any glaring discrepancies. We had a couple good conversations while he was there, and every point he tried to bring up in favor of vaccines, I had a good counter answer to, so much so, that he told me, that if he had to debate me on the subject at his medical school, I would definitely win the debate. Remember again, I am "just a mom", but I am a mom on a mission to not only help my son, but also others, if I can help it. I can read scientific studies just like anyone else.

Once you really start peeling back the layers of information, it doesn't take long to figure out that there definitely are a lot of questions when it comes to vaccines. Anyone who thinks they are completely safe should read up on the cases with our own government's vaccine injury court who as paid out over 4 BILLION dollars in damages for vaccine injuries since the late 1980's.

I could go on, but I will leave the rest of that topic for the experts to explain and for you to follow up on. Again, I will list some of my recommended reading at the end of my story, because I truly hope more people start taking the time to look deeper into the subject.

Chapter 15

An unexpected diagnosis

When we moved to Texas just after Jason turned six, we were fortunate enough that one of Jason's teachers told us that we needed to get Jason on the "list". I wasn't quite sure what the list was all about, but I called the phone number that they gave me and added Jason's name to the Texas Medicaid Waiver Waiting List. In South Texas, the place to call is Tropical Texas. They are an organization that works with the Texas Department of Disability and Aging to provide services to individuals with disabilities through different Medicaid waiver programs. Unfortunately, the waiting list for most of these waivers is around 14 or more years long.

There was one particular Medicaid program called Medically Dependent Children Program (MDCP) that was not based on our income. Jason's number came up for that particular program when he was around 13 years old. I didn't think his disability was severe enough to qualify him for the list, but miraculously, he was approved for the program. For the first time in Jason's life, he had Medicaid. We still carried private insurance for him through my husband's employer, but the Medicaid would cover whatever our private insurance didn't. After all these years, we could actually afford to start Jason back in private therapy. We got the referrals from his pediatrician and had evaluations done, and he qualified for speech, occupational and physical therapy.

Another great benefit of this program was that we had funds to hire someone to help with Jason. They called this respite care. My parents helped a lot with Jason, especially my dad, and we were able to officially hire him as Jason's respite aid. My parents would always help us without being paid, but it actually made me feel better to be able to compensate my dad for all that he did to help us with Jason. We could have hired anyone, but to be honest, we didn't know anyone who was available, whom we completely trusted with Jason's care. Taking care of a teenager with autism is not an easy job to begin with, and the fact that Jason was still mostly nonspeaking definitely made us much more hesitant to trust just anyone with his care.

For the first time in Jason's life, not only did we not have to juggle medical bills, but we could actually finally get him back into much needed therapies. The best part was that, for the most part, he actually enjoyed going to therapies. What a difference it was than when we used to take him during his early years and he would cry and fuss a lot.

It was during this time of being on the MDCP program that we had a meeting with the coordinator from Tropical Texas, where we had to go over all of Jason's medical information. As they took down the information regarding his autism and now epilepsy diagnosis, they also wanted to know his other diagnosis. I told them that was all I had, but they advised me to contact his orthopedic doctor, to ask him the diagnosis that lead to his SPML surgery and orthopedic braces that he wore on his legs. I was a little confused, because I had always attributed his toe walking and other orthopedic issues to be part of his autism. Let's face it, I had only met one kid with autism in my life before my own son, so I just mistakenly assumed everything that we dealt with fell under the autism diagnosis.

I made the call to the new orthopedic doctor we had recently started seeing and I spoke to his nurse. I told her I needed to know what was in Jason's file regarding why he wore braces on his legs. She found the file and read to me what was inside. His diagnosis was something along the lines of contracture of the legs and Cerebral Palsy. I almost dropped the phone when she said Cerebral Palsy. Never in Jason's 13 years of life had any doctor ever told me he had CP! I asked her if it truly did say in the file Cerebral Palsy and she confirmed it did. Even as I am writing this, I am still blown away from this experience.

Remember when I found studies when Jason was still a baby showing that infants who had bilirubin levels about 15 for three or more days had brain damage called kernicterus that is associated with Cerebral Palsy? Or when I used to jokingly say he ran like a kid that had CP because he would hold his arm and hand in a weird position as he ran. Then of course there was the doctor in Houston who performed the SPML surgery and he told me that he usually did this surgery for kids with CP. Somehow, all the signs were right there in front of me, but never once did any doctor EVER mention Cerebral Palsy!

I called a good friend of mine who was a physical therapist, and told her what I had learned. She thought it made sense. I couldn't understand how no doctor ever talked to me about Cerebral Palsy and she had a possible answer for that. She guessed that possibly these doctors may have thought it was something I already knew, especially since we didn't move to Texas until Jason was 6. When I had the next appointment with the orthopedic doctor, we discussed this diagnosis at length and he was also surprised no doctor had ever discussed it with me, especially since the SPML surgery is done for people who have CP.

Here I was with a 13- year old son who now had an additional diagnosis of Cerebral Palsy. This diagnosis answered so many questions for me. So many things that we dealt with in the first year of life with Jason were a result of his Cerebral Palsy. I always felt like the typical signs of autism really weren't there until later on, but at the same time Jason had so many developmental and feeding issues, and I didn't understand what was causing them. Now, I finally had another piece of the puzzle to better understand my son Jason.

It's hard now, as Jason ages to differentiate what is autism and what CP is in regards to what affects him overall. It is very clear though, that his balance issues and the slight deformity of his feet is definitely a result of the CP. He has severe learning issues and that is where the line gets a lot less clear, because either condition can be associated with that. All I know is that my son, despite his diagnosis, is truly my hero. He has had to work incredibly hard to get to the point where he is today.

Unfortunately for us, after a year on the MDCP program, the state said he no longer qualified for it. It made no sense because he still had the exact same issues that qualified him for it in the first place, along with the additional diagnosis that we didn't have before. We tried appealing the decision, but we were still denied. I wasn't ready to give up the Medicaid that easily though, and we put in an inquiry to see if we could possibly do a buy in, where we pay to have him on Medicaid. While that was being processed, he was able to continue on Medicaid. We continued with the therapies until about 18 months later, when we received word that Jason also did not qualify for the Medicaid buy in. The good news is because of him qualifying for the initial MDCP program, Jason was able to get 2 ½ years of therapy that we wouldn't be able to afford otherwise.

If you are a parent, especially in the state of Texas, who has a special needs child, please make sure you have their name added to the Medicaid Waiver waiting list. It doesn't matter if you understand what it is all about at this point. You will have years to figure it out, but the longer you wait to put them on that list, the longer you will wait for services. I have friends who didn't know about this list until their kids were almost 18. They are still waiting for services and their kids will most likely be in their 30's before they will ever qualify for these programs.

If your child is not on this list, please STOP reading right NOW and pick up the phone and make a call to add them. I'll be sure to add a phone number for reference at the end of this book and you can call it. I'm sure they can help refer you to the proper agency for the area you live in. (You can thank me later for this advice, just as I am so thankful someone shared the information with me all those years ago).

Chapter 16

Making lemonade
out of lemons

It's interesting, how something, that doesn't seem that significant at the time can truly change the course of your life. I had mentioned earlier, that I had gotten involved with the annual Autism Awareness Walk which was put on by our local school district. Getting involved with that also grew into coming up with teams so our local kids with disabilities had the opportunity to play baseball and soccer. I helped organize these programs along with our Director of Special Services and some of our other local parents, who helped coach. It was fun to see our kids out there having fun, but they pretty much were just playing against each other, except when we could find a team of other kids to come play with them. It never grew into much, but at least our kids had some opportunities that they had never had before.

My friend Nadine told me about a special prom that her church in the town of Brownsville was hosting for people with disabilities. She gave me the invitation with the information, in case I wanted to bring Jason. To be honest, I had thought about it, but the thought of going there when I didn't know anyone kind of put me out of my comfort zone. It doesn't help that our area is predominately Hispanic and, often, when I find myself hanging out with locals, a lot of the time they speak Spanish, so I am not really able to speak to them. I am bilingual, but my second language is German since both my parents immigrated to the US from Germany. My second language doesn't help me much in South Texas. It can be alienating to be parents of a child with special needs, but even more when there is a communication barrier with others. We often bowed out of invitations to not feel twice excluded.

I hadn't called to RSVP for the prom, but the day before I decided I would call and see if it wasn't too late to respond. Luckily, whoever I spoke with told me we could still attend, so I made plans to take Jason to his first prom at the age of 13. Jason did like music and he also liked lights, so he was pretty happy at the prom. I tried to get him to dance, but he was more interested in walking around the dance floor and hitting the decorations that were above his head. When I did try to get him on the dance floor, he just sat in a chair and watched me dance. Before I knew it, I was dancing with several of the other special guests at the prom and they were having so much fun! Their joy was contagious, and I left there really happy that we had come.

I had taken some pictures while we were there and I posted Jason's first prom pictures on Facebook. Some of Jason's teachers who were also my friends on Facebook, had commented that we should put on a prom in our town. Little did I know that the idea to host a prom would turn into years of opportunities for other kids and adults with disabilities. The four of us got together and planned a fundraising night to raise money to fund a prom. We did this first fundraiser at my house and tried to make it as nice as possible. The house we resided in at the time came with a baby grand piano, so I asked my friend Cristy to come and play the piano for us, while we had our wine and cheese prom fundraiser. She did and it helped make our first fundraiser a great success.

Our theme for the prom was A Night Under the Stars. I had come up with the idea, that people could sponsor stars of different values and sizes that would have their name on it, and we would hang them over the dance floor. The idea was a hit, and after our fundraiser night we had more than enough money to put on a prom for around 65 guests and their families. We even met with the city council in the town of Port Isabel, and they agreed to let us use their beautiful event center at no charge. This was an $1800 savings for us, which was a huge bonus.

We went all out and had everything decorated, centerpieces, table cloths, a DJ for music and a photographer to take prom pictures. After all the planning and preparation, we all teared up seeing our beautiful guests of honor arrive. It was an amazing experience for everyone and, we decided we should make the prom an annual event.

We were very careful in how we spent our money, and because of that, we had money left over. We decided to use the money to put on a special Candyland Christmas party for all the special needs kids from our school district. We worked ahead of time on decorations including wood structures of large lollipops, a giant snowman and also gingerbread men. We had a team of volunteers ready to help us set up and, of course, we had Santa scheduled to arrive on a fire truck to bring presents.

We planned for everything, except for a sudden change in the weather. The forecast for that day was showing that a cold front would blow through. We lived in South Texas, and it never really gets that cold here, so we just figured that everyone might need to wear a coat. A typical December cold front means that the temps drop from the high 70's to the low 70's. We all showed up at the park 2 hours before the event to set up, but after we got there, we got word from a local police officer that there were winds of 70 mph forecast to come through with this front which was going to arrive during our event. Cold we could deal with, but dangerous winds were another story.

We knew we had so many kids and families planning on attending that the last thing I wanted to do was to disappoint them. It was also difficult to get word to them about any changes. Since I lived on the same street as the park, I made the very last-minute decision to move the entire event to my house. My husband was definitely taken by surprise when I showed up at the house with my team and a group of volunteers. I told him we had to do the party at our house and I didn't give him any other option. In 2 hours, we had transformed my garage and house into a Christmas Candyland. We covered a lot of our garage walls with wrapping paper and had the special huge chair that we had set up for Santa. We had a large living room, the same room with the piano that we used earlier in the summer. I pushed all the furniture to one side of the room and lined up tables that were covered with candy and snacks. We even had tons of cakes donated for a cake walk, so our kitchen counters were covered with the cakes and we did the cake walk around our dining room table. We had a long driveway, so there was a lot of room for the kids to run around. We even had a little train, which was pulled by a riding mower that the kids could ride on.

We did have a visit from the police department but not due to weather. We had too many cars blocking the road, and they couldn't get through with the firetruck to bring Santa, until everyone moved their vehicles. We also had a little mix up with the tables that we took from the park. I thought they were brought out by one of our team members, but it turns out they were dropped off for an event happening the next morning, so they were reported as stolen. Oops! Fortunately, we got everything sorted out, and we were able to borrow the tables for our event and return them to the park after.

It was complete chaos, but our kids had so much fun! Nothing beats seeing our kids happy, but we as parents know that many events put on for kids often can be overwhelming for our kids. Our event was a safe place where our kids were free to be who they were, without anyone questioning their behavior or why they may look a little different.

The next Spring, when I helped again with the Autism Walk, our group was in charge of having the shirts for the walk made. We found some sponsors to help with the cost of the shirts, and we used the proceeds to keep funding activities for our kids. At the time, there were very little opportunities for kids with special needs around, so even though we were doing these events, I always wished there would be more opportunities for our kids.

We had moved again during that year. (I could write an entire book just about all of our moves!) Because of the move, I needed a new location to do our annual prom fundraiser. We had moved back to the golf course community that we had previously lived in. My friend, Cristina, suggested that she could help me with the food if I wanted to do the fundraiser at the restaurant in our neighborhood. The fundraiser went well, and this time we added items for people to bid on at a silent auction. Once again, we raised more than enough money for our next prom, and we kept expanding on helping to provide programs and support for our special-needs community. At the end of the year, we collected wish-lists from our special ed teachers, and we were able to purchase much needed items for their classrooms.

It was really pretty awesome to not only be able to do things that would help Jason, but also help all his classmates and other students from our community and beyond. That second year, we were smart enough to plan ahead when it came to our Christmas event, and we held it at the home owners clubhouse in our neighborhood. At that time, the event was still just for kids from our school district. We definitely filled the room up with our activities and, of course, the special visit from our Santa. That year, we even had enough funds to spend a little more on presents for the kids. We got their wish list ahead of time, and Santa brought in wrapped gifts that were picked out especially for them.

As time went on, I really saw the need to be able to reach out to our special-needs community in neighboring cities. Our prom drew in adolescents and adults from our entire county the 2nd year, and we had around 85 special needs individuals there with their parents or caregivers. I knew that I really wanted to expand on what we were doing, but I was the main one doing a lot of the legwork and running around at that time. My friend Wendi helped me for a time when she could, but often I was spending a lot of hours making everything happen. The team that I started with still helped when they could, but they all worked full time jobs and just didn't have the time to put into it. I knew if I was to be able to do more, I would need some help, so I started paying more attention to what other organizations in neighboring counties were doing.

I had actually met with one mom named Deborah, who was doing great things for the Down Syndrome community. We talked about how she ran things, and even though what I was doing wouldn't quite fit with her organization, she mentioned the name of another organization that I should check out, called the Capable Kids Foundation. I made it a point to learn more about them and that suggestion went on to change so many things for the better.

Chapter 17

The later teen years

When Jason was around 13 years old, we made the difficult decision to put the beautiful house we had built on the market. It was a great house, but it had a big problem that we didn't realize until it was too late. It would occasionally be in the path of oncoming golf balls. Not being golfers ourselves, we didn't realize that this would be a problem, especially since it was so far from where golfers would tee off and nowhere in the path of where the golfers were aiming for. We had even spent the money to purchase larger trees to hopefully block the path of random stray balls, but unfortunately, we had a very unusual hard freeze that winter that killed all the trees and left us even more exposed than ever. Jason's room was on the second story of our house and the 3rd time a golf ball came crashing through his window, we knew that this house would not work out for us long term. Add to the fact that when Jason was in the backyard, he would never even pay attention if there were golfers on the course, there was no easy way to make sure he would be safe.

We sold the house relatively quickly, but at the time, we hadn't been able to find another house to purchase. We ended up moving into a rental home until we could find something on the market that would work. The nice thing about the rental house was that it was just a block away from my parent's house, so we had help just around the corner. After around 6 months, we found a house outside of the golf course neighborhood that we liked and ended up purchasing it. After dealing with the golf ball issue for two years, I was happy to be nowhere near a golf course.

Jason and Dylan had been sharing a room ever since we added their sister Kimberly to the family, and even though they would need to continue sharing, their new room was definitely bigger than their last room. Dylan was also getting closer to graduating, so we knew that soon he would be moving on and moving out, so there was no reason to look for an extra bedroom. The house we were buying was a large one-story house that had been built in the early 70's. What we loved about it was that it had a huge walled in backyard along with the necessary pool for Jason to play in. No possibility of random golf balls to come crashing through the yard.

This was the house where we would end up doing the last-minute Christmas event for our kids at, because it was right down the street from the park. This was also the house where we did our very first wine and cheese fundraiser party. We really enjoyed so many aspects of this house, and for a while it was a great fit.

As time went on, Dylan graduated high school and after considering his options, he decided to join the Air Force. He had always known that we did not have a college savings fund for him, because for many years we were just trying to keep up with all the medical bills. Scott had been in the Air Force when we first met, and many members of our family have also served in the military, so for Dylan it was a great choice.

I knew it would be hard on Jason to have his brother leave home, but I think it was even more difficult that, when he left, there was a long period of time where Jason wouldn't have any contact with him at all. Jason was definitely confused during this time, and he always kept asking when Dylan was coming home. We were able to go as a family to Dylan's graduation from basic training, and it was Jason's first opportunity to see where Dylan had been living. He couldn't take his eyes off his brother that weekend. They really had and still do have a very special bond. A couple years later Dylan would get his first and so far, only tattoo. It is a very simple puzzle piece that he had done on his forearm in honor of his brother. Not too long later, their sister Kimberly would also get a matching tattoo.

Dylan has been in the Air Force for almost 4 years now and Jason still asks almost daily when Dylan is coming home. Dylan usually makes it home a couple times a year, and we have been up to see him a couple times. He is stationed in Nebraska, so it's not an area that we would normally go to, and it definitely it too far to drive to very easily. We do facetime calls occasionally so Jason gets to see his big brother. Jason has never been one to talk on the phone, so he is always happiest when his brother actually comes back home for a visit.

A year after Dylan left home, Kimberly graduated and also moved out on her own. She started college and moved into the dorms about 40 minutes away from our town. Life changed so fast for all of us with two kids moving out within two years. Jason definitely took all the changes the hardest. It was also harder for us, because we no longer had extra sets of eyes to watch out for Jason.

As much as we loved our house with the walled in backyard, the layout of it was pretty spread out, which meant it was hard to keep a constant eye on Jason. We didn't have to worry so much of him wandering off as he did in his early years, but he was a very curious kid who could quickly destroy something within minutes. An example of this was our rose garden that we had on one side of our house. I would work hard to keep it pruned so we would continually have beautiful flowers. One day, I went in the backyard to check on Jason, who had been outside for maybe 10 minutes max, and my entire rose garden was cut almost down to the ground. Jason proudly used his words and told me "I cut the tree".

Another time Scott and I were watching television in Scott's new "man cave", which was Kimberly's former bedroom. Suddenly, the smoke detectors started going off. I ran down the hall and turned the corner to the living room to see all the smoke. When I made it to the kitchen, Jason was standing there with a puzzled look on his face, because he had no idea what was going on. It turned out that he had started a fire in the microwave by cooking a corndog. I'm pretty sure that, instead of hitting the button for one minute, he accidentally hit the button twice and set the microwave for 11 minutes.

Incidents like that, along with a few other issues, made us realize that this house may not be the best house for us for the long term with Jason. We needed a smaller house, where we would be able to keep a close eye on him. Not having his brother and sister around to help definitely was a big wake up call for us. We were no strangers to moving, so we once again put our house on the market with a new goal in mind, a safer house for Jason.

In the end, we received an offer the first week that our house was on the market. A few months later we purchased our next house, which is the house we are still in today. It was back in the golf course neighborhood, but this time we are at the part of the golf course where the golfers tee off, so there is no chance of ever having a ball go into our yard. Our house is much smaller, so from the kitchen we can see the door into every room in the house as well as most of the backyard. Being much smaller also means we hear Jason's TV, music, and iPad too, but it is what is necessary in order to be able to make sure he is safe.

Now that Jason is 18, I'd love for him to be able to be more independent and be able to be home alone, but we just aren't at that point yet. He still has very little concept of things that can be dangerous, and because of that he still requires constant supervision. I'm hoping one of these days to be able to install cameras so I don't have to always have him within my sight. It does get tiring after all these years to have to still keep an eye on him, but in just minutes, he can destroy things or get into things he shouldn't, and the only way to stop him is to be there.

I am thankful that I am in a position where I still can work my life around him. Even with all my activities I do for our special-needs kids, I can take him with me to almost everything I do. I look at it as on the job training for him. He has become my helper. He helps me carry things to events and even sits at the informational tables that we do.

Now that he has officially graduated from high school, he will start the next phase of his education, which will be more focused on job training and building of his life skills, to continue help him to be more independent.

We also have a new avenue medically that we are about to embark on. In the fall of last year, we transitioned Jason to a new doctor, knowing he had outgrown his pediatrician. Jason is now 6' 3", and taller than any of his doctors or staff. We decided to take him to the new local clinic that opened up in our town, and we did all the standard blood tests that they do for all their new patients. Surprisingly, something showed up on one of his blood tests that required him to come back to do another one. After all these years of going to doctors in search of answers; here at a little clinic run by the local university, they stumbled onto an important finding: Jason's bilirubin count was still elevated!

The last time Jason had a doctor check his bilirubin, he was 2 months old and at that time it registered just over 3. The retired cardiologist I recently met, told me that even back then that should have been a red flag; but just like so many other red flags for Jason, that one was also missed. Now, we are finding out that Jason has gone his entire life with this condition that definitely plays a role in how his body processes certain medications. The doctor wants to send him to some specialists and do more testing.

They don't think his condition is life threatening, but it is an important thing that we need to follow up on. I look at it as just one more piece of the puzzle that might help explain why Jason has had severe reactions to certain things over the years.

Because Jason just turned 18, he will now be able to qualify for Medicaid, which will help as we once again start seeing more doctors to find out more about what is going on with his liver. It most likely will be something that there is no treatment for, but it will be important to know more, in case there is ever the time that he requires medication for anything in the future. I look at it as just one more step on this lifetime journey to help Jason any way we can.

Chapter 18

Capable Kids Foundation Lower Valley

As I've stated before, we went through many struggles with Jason over the years. It took years to before we were able to eat in a restaurant and not be completely exhausted after, or at the very least, not have to deal with stares from people who noticed Jason's behavior. Jason is a good kid, but he does have autism. Some people who have autism have been able to express what they go through. They often explain that they feel as if they don't have control of their bodies. They might make loud noises or hit themselves even though they don't want to. It is difficult for them and, honestly it is difficult for us as a family, because we often feel the stares and annoyance of people who don't understand our kids.

As much as we would love for our kids to participate in regular school activities or city sports programs, for many of our kids that just isn't an option. I have seen families try and for the most part, it doesn't work out. That's not to say that some kids are now able to adjust and participate. We have some kids in our programs that have the physical skills to compete in sports, but they might be affected by other issues that make participating difficult.

In my effort to expand on what we were already doing locally, I looked into the Capable Kids Foundation that was based out of a neighboring county, about an hour away. I saw that they were about to start a football season for their kids. Despite the distance, I signed Jason up to participate. He loved football and had never had the opportunity to play.

Once a week, we drove around 120 miles round trip and watched Jason play football for about 45 minutes. The game was completely modified so our kids would be able to have fun. It was also played indoors. The very first time Jason was given the ball, he started running towards the end zone. One of the kids tagged him on his shoulder and, since it was tag football, Jason stopped, but he also started crying loudly. The poor kid that had tagged him stepped back because I think he thought maybe he had hurt Jason. As soon as Jason saw that the kid stepped back, Jason took off running again to score a touchdown. It was pretty hilarious to watch and I knew at that moment that Jason would enjoy this new version of football.

Jason actually cried off and on the first two practices/games, but by the third week, he was just out there having a great time. New experiences can sometimes be overwhelming for him, and that is where the tears can come from. Those 4 weeks went by quickly, but at least over that time I was also able to get a good idea of what the Capable Kids Foundation was all about. They basically were doing some of the things we were doing on our side of the valley, but on a much larger scale.

I reached out to the Executive Director, Esmer Leal, and told her about what we were doing in my area and asked if she thought there was a chance for my group to join hers. I was willing to still do our own fundraising as much as possible, but what I really needed help with was the organizational side of things. It's one thing to raise money for programs, it's a totally different thing to make sure everything is done correctly in terms of the IRS. My organization was considered a not for profit, but we were not an official nonprofit. I was willing to work hard, but I really needed the help of someone who had more experience and resources to successfully grow our programs to reach more kids and young adults.

Esmer gave me the opportunity to meet with the board members. The board approved adding a new division of Capable Kids. We would be known as Capable Kids Foundation Lower Valley. Our previous group name was Lower Valley Event Committee, so we kept the Lower Valley and just added the Capable Kids.

Initially, things didn't appear to change much just because we were now part of Capable Kids. I still ran everything out of my home office that was always a complete disaster area. From the first prom alone, I had 80 table cloths that were stored all over my house, plus tons of other supplies. I kept everything and anything that we could possibly use again. Some items were too big to store at home, so I had to get a small storage unit to store the wood structures and sporting equipment. Somethings though, could not be put in storage because of our high humidity. I even started storing things in bins under my bed. My husband was increasingly suggesting we needed to find an office, but at that time there were not enough funds to make that happen. He also was suggesting I needed to get paid, but that was even less likely to happen.

Don't get me wrong, my husband, Scott, was very supportive of what I was doing, but at the end of the day he didn't want to have to come home to see all my work paraphernalia everywhere. I don't blame him .As much as I tried to keep things organized, it was almost impossible in the space I had to work with.

There was one bright spot, though, when it came to getting paid, I found a way to make money from home. We had a small pool house behind our newest house. Originally, it was meant to be Jason's TV and toy area, but after a few months, he started moving all of his toys back into our house. Since Jason was no longer using the space, I decided to turn it into a vacation rental on Airbnb. I had a part time job helping my friend Jan do the books and manage her many vacation rentals on South Padre Island, so I was confident I could make this work.

I invested a little money in furnishings, bedding and towels, and Casita del Sol was launched. At first, we just had bookings over Spring Break and summer weekends, but by the second year, we were booked almost solid all summer and now in our 3rd year, we have pretty steady business from mid-January on-so much so, that now I have to block out dates when Dylan comes home to visit or when we have family or friends visit.

I have been part of Capable Kids Lower Valley for two years now and about 6 months ago, we finally found an affordable small office space with an air-conditioned storage unit. It was a great day in our house when I could move everything to our office. I was looking forward to finally having a little extra space in the house, but literally by the time I got home from moving everything, Jason had moved ALL of his toys from his room into my former office, and he claimed the room for himself.

Things still aren't at a point where I am able to get paid for what I do for our special-needs community, but to be honest, as much as extra income would come in handy, I absolutely love what I am doing!

We have done 2 more proms as part of the Capable Kids Foundation, for a total of 4 so far. We are in the very beginning phase of planning our next prom, which will be a little different this year. I figure we have done 4 formal proms, and it's time to change it up. My entire focus is to give our kids and young adults new opportunities and the idea for the next time is an 80's theme dance. I was a teenager in the 80's and I have some very fond memories of the music and fashions of those years.

I always want to do more events and I do have a little more help now, including part time assistant Julissa, who does all the time consuming and tedious computer work and bookkeeping. I still get some great help from the now former Executive Director Esmer, and the new Interim Executive Director Evelyn Cano. I also have a few more parents who are getting involved and helping me with our events and programs. I tend to be a little of a control freak, so it does take me time to be ok to let people help more, but I know that at this point it is definitely necessary. I do still have to balance things at home though, so sometimes I have to be ok with taking a little time for myself and my family.

We have been able to bring so many new opportunities and events to our local community over the past few years. The best part is, to see our kids have so much fun. It is also heartwarming to see their families get to cheer for them and watch them participate in events that might not have been possible just a few years ago. The list of what we have been able to do is too long to list, but in addition to proms and sports, some of the other activities include surfing clinics, fishing, and painting.

Sometimes dealing with the reality of having a child with special needs can be overwhelming. Fortunately for me, those days are fewer and further between. I am so thankful for that one invitation from our Special Ed Director Elsa, who invited me to help plan the first autism walk. Had it not been for her, I really don't know if I would have ever built up the confidence to not only help plan events, but get to the point where I am completely in charge of them and also to be a spokesperson at times for individuals with disabilities. Who would have believed, that someone like me who would feel like passing out at the thought of speaking in front of people, is now comfortable to speak in front of hundreds of people? I have been given the honor of being a voice for my son and his friends. I will continue to do what I can to help give them the full life that they deserve.

Chapter 19

Grief and Guilt

I think many parents of kids with disabilities, me included, often deal with being in in a state of grief or in a state of guilt. The grief is for our child never being able to live the life that we dreamed for them to have. I never dreamed my son at 18 would need me to shave his face for him or help him brush his teeth properly.

For years, I have known that one day when Jason turned 18, he would be able to apply for Social Security benefits. Again, not one of those things you dream about doing for your adult child, but at this point in Jason's life, it is the reality of what we must face. We need to make sure that Jason can be taken care of now that he is an adult.

When we went to apply for benefits at the Social Security office, we came prepared with lots of documentation. We sat and waited the mandatory couple hours before being called for our turn. The nice man helping us needed to start by asking Jason a few simple questions. The questions were as follows:

- Do you have a job?
- Are you married?
- Do you live with your mom and dad?

Jason's answer to all three of those questions was a resounding "yes". It actually was a little funny at the time hearing Jason say he had a job and was married, but at the end of the day when I try to go to sleep at night, those same words that made me laugh earlier in the day bring me to tears at night. It's brings back that dreaded grief that I, am usually very good at ignoring.

Here we are, 18 years into this journey and it is still challenging to handle our reality. Some days, though, it still hits me like a ton of bricks. I think it was a little easier during the childhood years, because of course it's my job as a parent to take care of the needs of my child. It is a very normal state to live with.

Having your child turn 18 though, brings a new set of circumstances into our life. Our son is now legally an adult. He even received his selective service card in the mail recently which means if there is ever a draft, they might call him up. We had to have our son sign paperwork giving us, his parents, permission to help him make decisions. Without that paperwork, the school and doctor cannot speak to us about Jason.

That first question that Jason answered yes to, about having a job, for many other kids, the standard answer should be yes. I wish it truly could be a yes answer for Jason, but the reality is that he is no-where near ready to be able to be employed. He will start working with a job coach during the next school year and we are hopeful he can learn some job skills. Of course, there is the other sad reality and that is, even if he is able to learn and perform some type of job, he is only allowed to make a minimal amount of money or he will lose his Social Security and Medicaid benefits. The chance of Jason ever being able to earn a wage that he could live on is not realistic, given his current abilities. I don't want to ever limit my son, but I also do have to look at reality. "Reality," is a word that I use often because there's no way to avoid it.

The second question- "Are you married?" Even though I wouldn't want any of my kids to be married at age 18, the fact is, once again, the chances of Jason ever getting married are also not very realistic. There is no question that he likes girls, but at the same time he doesn't know how to communicate with them, let alone have a relationship with them.

Tonight, is one of those nights where the grief that I felt all those years ago has reared its ugly head up again to remind me of more things that my beautiful son will most likely miss out on in life. It is sad, and some nights like tonight, I will take my time to silently cry while everyone else in the house is sleeping.

I don't write about this so people will feel sorry for us. I write about this so people who don't have children with disabilities get a little better understanding of what us special needs parents go through. If you ever want to bring a special needs parent to tears almost instantly, just ask them what they will do with their child when they are too old or too sick to take care of them themselves. It's another one of those things that keeps us up at night.

I don't fault people for attempting to think they understand, but unless you live in our shoes, you will never know the true heartbreak that we live with every day of our lives. We might do a good job of pushing past it and living each day as it comes, but it is always there just below the surface, ready to bring us to our knees in tears.

As I was having to answer so many questions today about Jason's life and medical background, it also brought on those horrible feelings of guilt. I had to list every doctor that I could recall, so that the government can request the medical records. As I had to detail some of Jason's history, I felt the need to explain that I tried to get the doctors to help him, but they wouldn't listen to me. It once again reminded me of how I had failed to protect my son from harm when he was a baby.

If I only knew then what I know now, how differently a day like today would have been. Had I had the knowledge to tell the doctor that Jason's bilirubin levels were at a critical level and demand that it be addressed immediately, he might have never missed all his milestones his first 4 months. If I had realized that his nonstop screaming for almost 4 months was most likely an adverse vaccine reaction, I would have known that he needed further testing to see if he was genetically predisposed to possible reactions, thus forgoing his future vaccines and not having to live with the damage that they would cause his developing brain and body.

Yes, the guilt is real. Even though I can try to justify it away by saying that his doctors ultimately should bare the blame for at the very least not informing me of the possible adverse side effects, but also for not recognizing them when they did happen. At the end of the day, I am the mom and I will always bare the ultimate responsibility for not protecting my child enough.

I think it is because of this that I have become a lot more vocal about the risks of vaccines. I know first-hand how most doctors fail to tell the truth to parents or even give them the option to know there is a choice when it comes to vaccines. Almost daily, I see stories of another baby or child injured or killed because of a vaccine. It just reminds me of how important it is to do what I can do, so I can possibly spare someone from having to deal with the very real possibility of adverse vaccine reactions.

I still remember back when Jason had his seizure how the doctor told me that 30% of kids who have autism also develop epilepsy. He said that if they didn't have epilepsy as a young child, sometimes they develop it when they reach puberty. I really wonder if there is a link to possible medication or vaccines for the ones who have the later onset of epilepsy like my son developed. Jason has been completely off of any medication for years now and has never had another seizure.

The logical side of me does understand that the doctors truly did fail my child, and I only did what any parent thinks is best for their child. It's the emotional side of me that stays up at night wondering if there is anything I missed or could still possibly do to help my son.

So, there you have it, guilt and grief all carried around silently while we do the best that we can. I know that this is not the most uplifting chapter of this book, but at the end of the day, I want to address the good, bad and the ugly of what this journey is like, because I truly want other parents who go through the same emotions to know that they are not alone.

Chapter 20

Support Matters

At this point in my life, I often meet or speak to many other families who are also navigating through life with their special-needs child. One thing I hear often is how many of them don't get any help from their immediate family. I realize not all families are created equal, but it truly makes me sad knowing not only how much more challenging their journey may be, but also sad that their family is missing out on having a relationship with this child. No matter what the disability is, I honestly do not ever recall meeting a special needs child that has not enriched my life in some way. We truly can learn so much from them!

That being said, I know sometimes it is challenging to take care of a child with a disability, but at the end of the day, I would hope that those family bonds can be strong enough to extend love and support to all of their family members of all abilities. Daily life for us special needs families can often be stressful and exhausting. I just want to encourage extended family members to take a more active role in being more involved if they aren't already. Even one evening or afternoon a month of giving a family a break can make such a difference. You would be surprised at how many parents haven't had a real break for years.

I truly have been abundantly blessed through the years to have so much support from my family when it came to all my kids. My dad especially has always had a special bond with Jason, and I know that was the main reason why my parents decided to relocate from Washington to Texas. Back when my father was battling cancer, he was at peace with dying, but the one thing that broke his heart was to not be there for Jason. I truly think his desire to help with Jason helped give him the extra strength he needed to fight and win his battle with cancer.

My in laws were around in the very early years to help, but they are habitual movers like us and have moved many times since then. They did move to Texas for a short time, but found that they missed living on a sailboat too much to stay living in a house, so shortly after they moved here, they moved on again.

Living with a child with a disability can often feel very isolating. It's so much more difficult to keep up with old friendships when your child no longer fits into the regular play groups with other kids. I think friends want to be there, but sometimes they don't know what to say or what to do, so over time they slowly lose contact, because they don't have things in common like they used to. Their kids also have less in common, which also makes maintaining the friendship that much more difficult. People get busy with their own lives, and I don't fault them for it. I know the journey that we are on with Jason is very different than that of families whose kids have grown up and moved on.

No matter if you have family support or not, I think it is so important to find other families in the area that you can connect with. I know it took many years for me to get to know other special needs families when I moved here to Texas. In the small town that we're in, many of Jason's classmate's families have lived here for generations. They weren't looking to make new friends, because they already had lots of local friends and family. We've lived here long enough though. that we were able to get to become friends with the other families, and it is always great to run into them around town.

Many communities are having support groups start up. If you aren't sure where to find them, check with your local therapy clinics or schools to see if they know of any. If there aren't any, then maybe start your own. It could be as simple as picking one day a month to do a playdate at the park or coffee at a local restaurant. From personal experience, I know there are always families looking for support.

I looked for a support group when I first moved to Texas, but the only one I could find was around 40 minutes away and only for people who spoke Spanish. Back when we had our former Special Ed Director, she did organize a few support group meetings that I was involved in, but once she left our district, those meetings ended.

Once I became part of Capable Kids Foundation, I found a church willing to open up their doors to let us have our support group meetings. You would think that most churches would be willing to help with something like this, but I found that not to be the case. I was looking for a church that would be more in a centrally located area, so my home church was not an option. I was very thankful to finally find a location, so that our families could meet once a month. We recently moved our meetings to a new church that is more in the area that I was originally hoping for. The first location was a good 45 minutes away from where I live. Our new location is only 25 minutes away and also just down the street from our office. It is definitely much easier for me to get to.

During our meetings, we bring in different speakers to inform us on a wide range of topics that we as families need to learn. It seems that the information we need to know as special needs parents is endless. From navigating through the school process, to dealing with insurance, or what to do when our kids reach adulthood, is all information that we need to know to best help our kids. Sometimes we take a break and just have a good old-fashioned potluck and share our stories and experiences.

There is so much to learn along the way, that it is so much easier when you can talk to other families going through similar things. We all have so much we can learn from each other. This journey is definitely too tough to try to do alone. Trust me, I've tried that and it is so much better when you have someone else to talk to.

Chapter 21

Day to Day Life

I meet parents all the time who struggle with daily life with their kids. It's one thing to have our kids at home or with family, because it's a familiar environment. In our own homes, there aren't people who will judge our kids or give them weird looks. Going out in public with our kids though can often not be so easy.

Many parents have very similar experiences to mine, when it comes to taking their children out. In the earlier years, it was especially difficult for us to go most places. There was a very long period of time when we no longer went to church. It wasn't because we didn't want to, but because truly there was not a church that was a good fit for Jason.

We had found a church that we did like after we moved to Texas. It would take about 25 minutes to get there from our house. Jason loved going in the nursery while we were able to enjoy the service. Unfortunately, after a few weeks of going there, we were told that if you put your child in the nursery, you were required to volunteer in the nursery once a month. Just getting to church in the morning was at that time a huge undertaking. To go through all that and not be able to attend a service, was just too much for us at the time, and we decided that the church was not going to be the right fit for us after all.

Sometimes, we would try to watch some church services on TV at home, but it never was that easy either. At home there were always so many distractions. I know for me personally, I really missed being able to be part of the church family. Through the years, occasionally we would visit the church my parents were attending, because our older son Dylan would be invited to play his trumpet for a special song during the service. We would go, but most of the service I would be focused on trying to keep Jason quiet. After maybe the third time of going to my parent's church, I received a phone call from the church secretary, who was also the choir director. He called to see if we may be interested in attending church with them. Apparently, they had a discussion at church and several members wanted to help. They would have somebody who would sit with Jason in the church dining area and play with him during the service. Even as I write this, it still makes me tear up thinking about that call. As a Christian, I feel it is our duty to reach out to those in need. I know that we are all only human, and I don't fault people for sometimes failing to reach out.

This call truly reminded me that there are people out there who want to serve and help others. I don't think a lot of people give much thought to families who have children with disabilities, possibly because it's not something they think about. They don't realize how just a small gesture of offering help for one hour a week during a church service can mean so much.

At this church, there were five different congregation members who signed up to take one Sunday a month to sit with Jason so that we could attend church again. Because of this accommodation, we were able to become members of a church. Jason loved going and loved playing in the back. Over time, they would also bring him out for the children sermon. Once he realized that he liked that portion of church service, he decided that he did not want to go in the back room after the children sermon, and he would come and sit with us instead. He was not always quiet, but at least we had almost half the service where we could really enjoy it without having to worry about taking care of him at the same time. Over time, Jason got to the point where he wanted to be in the service with us the entire time. Often, he would sit with my parents and I loved that, because then I could truly enjoy the service. We still attend that church. Life has gotten a lot busier, so we can't attend services as often as we used to but, we definitely will always appreciate that call inviting us to come and be part of their church family.

If you can grasp how challenging it was to just attend church, then maybe you can also understand how much more difficult almost every regular day activity could be for not only our family, but thousands of others like ours. Restaurants were one of the hardest things to go to. Having to sit in a seat for a long period of time was never easy for Jason. Just like church, there were several years where we avoided eating out, because it was mentally and physically exhausting. We limited our eating out to fast food places for many years. Over time, as Jason was able to better handle the noise and activity of fast food restaurants, we slowly reintroduced regular restaurants to him. It has taken many years of practice to finally get to the point where Jason does quite well in restaurants. It was worth all the stress we had to go through to get to this point, because it gives us so many more options.

Stores in general have been challenging over the years. For as long as I could lift Jason, I used to always put him inside the cart, so I wouldn't have to chase him around the store. Eventually he got too big for the cart and I would do my best to have him help me push the cart in order to keep him close by. Of course, if there was something he wanted to see, in just seconds, he would take off down an aisle. His two favorite places of our local Walmart are the toy section and the section that has vacuum and steam cleaners. Despite the fact that we own both, he often would try to load new ones in my cart.

The benefits to living in a small town are that many of store staff now know Jason. Often, if he is seen without me nearby, they keep a close eye on him until they see that I have found him. At 6 foot 3 inches, he can move across the store pretty fast. I don't worry about him quite as much as I used to, because I know he won't leave the aisles of the store that he loves. Even so, I still do my best to be close by, because other people don't know him and may not understand his behavior.

Two other places Jason likes to go are the beach and the zoo. At the beach, we do our best to try to be a little bit away from the other beachgoers. I can't tell you how many times Jason has seen another child's beach toy and just sat down and started playing with it. Those instances are always followed by me having to explain that he has autism. For the most part, we have met mostly nice people when this has happened. It is amazing, over the years, how the conversations have changed from having to explain what autism is, to now most people telling me that they either know kids with autism or have a family member with autism.

When we go to the zoo, Jason's favorite activity is to run through the park as fast as possible in order to make it to the playground. It has taken years to get him to slow down and

Stephanie K. Wilson

actually pay attention to the animals. He now likes visiting the petting zoo area and also feeding the giraffes. We still have to stop him from trying to chase and scare the birds though. For some reason, he loves trying to make birds fly away.

Scott and I love going to the movies, and for many years it was a huge struggle to be able to take Jason. Not only would he make a lot of noise and sometimes throw popcorn or napkins through the air, but he also would need about 4 or 5 visits to the bathroom during the movie. Between a combination of us and his school taking him to the movies over and over, he can now sit through an entire movie. For the most part, he is quiet, but if it is a funny movie, his laughs and reactions are usually louder than most other people in the theater. He doesn't seem to get too excited to go to the movies, but we do take him anyway. I think he knows how much work it is for him to be able to sit and be quiet for so long, so it isn't anything he seeks out to do. Usually, once he is there though, we can see that he does enjoy it.

Pretty much everywhere we go with Jason can be a more challenging experience than most people normally deal with. The great thing through the years is that he really has gotten so much easier to go out with. It didn't happen overnight, but I am truly proud of the progress he has made. I now even have him accompany me as my assistant when I visit businesses and ask them for donations for our fundraiser events. I love that, even though I may not know many of the people working in the businesses, many of them actually know Jason. He is actually one of those kids that is easy to recognize. The hardest part for me is that, even if Jason does know them, he doesn't have the verbal skills to tell me who they are.

I am proud to carry the title of Jason's mom around town. He really has made an impact on our community and helped bring kids like him and his classmates to the attention of others. At the end of the day, we want our kids to be welcome everywhere they go. They deserve to have the opportunity to experience life, just like everyone else. As a parent, I do my best to have him behave and be respectful of where he is at, but at the same time, sometimes he may still act up. I really hope one day that our society sees our kids as we do, maybe a little different, but definitely not less. A little compassion and patience can go a long way into making trips out in public a little less stressful.

Chapter 22

A Little Something About Jason

At this point, I know I have written quite a lot about our journey with Jason, but I don't really think I have really introduced you to our amazing son. When I think of Jason, a smile comes to my face and tears come to my eyes. I know all of our kids impact our lives in many ways, but Jason is one of those kids who people really remember. I often refer to him as my giant child. He's 6'3" and somewhere around 155 pounds. He possibly could be a little taller, but he doesn't stay still long enough for me to measure him.

Even though Jason is a boy of few words, he is nowhere near a quiet person. He is almost constantly making some type of noise. He loves speaking to his dog and cats, and you would think as much as he speaks to them, that they must be answering back. He also loves speaking to my parent's parrot. He mimics the sounds so well, that sometimes it's hard to tell if it is the bird making the sound or Jason.

Jason is at his happiest when he pulls our standard poodle Brittney to lay on top of him. Brittney is the most patient dog in the world and pretty much will do whatever Jason wants. Of our many cats we have had over the years, we finally have one who will let Jason hold her. I think it helps that she is the only one who still has her front claws.

Jason also loves making animal sounds. In fact, he picks up on sounds that I think most of us don't notice. We can be outside and he may hear a bird or even an airplane off in the distance and he will start mimicking the noise he is hearing. Speaking of airplanes, Jason loves playing with small airplanes, and if he doesn't have one in his pocket, he pretends his hand is an airplane, and he can often be seen walking through the store or the parking lot with his hand high in the air flying his make-believe airplane. Depending on the place, we sometimes encourage him to "land the airplane" to help avoid stares from people who have no idea what he is doing. It is a soothing thing for Jason though, so we don't stop him nearly as much as we used to. Sometimes he's so focused on "flying his plane" though that he doesn't pay attention to where he's walking, so it has become a safety issue at times. One time he was so busy flying his plane that he knocked an entire tub of popcorn out of someone's hands when we were at the movie theater.

Since early on, Jason has loved trains. He has had probably almost every Thomas Train over the years, including the type that go on the wooden tracks, as well as the plastic tracks, and of course the cute mini trains that came out a few years ago. The first thing Jason wants to get when we go to a store is more train tracks. We finally have stopped buying them because we honestly don't have any more room to store them. It is really great to see the configurations of tracks that Jason builds. He can take over an entire room with them and sometimes will expand out the door into the next room, if I let him. We are often having to step over his toys in our house.

Some other things Jason has really gotten into playing with over the years are blocks and dominos. He builds intricate mazes and structures with them. I remember him having many issues with his fine motor skills when he was younger, but now he definitely has mastered control of his hands. We often take pictures of his creations, because even if he takes an hour to build it, when he's done, he enjoys knocking it down. He also loves drawing. For the past few years, many of his drawings are either of roller coasters (which he will not go on) or they are of house plans that include the schematics for a central vacuum system. Not your average type drawings that most kids do, but Jason has probably drawn hundreds of these over the years.

Jason does like spending time on his iPad too. He usually is either watching videos of all kinds or he likes to browse Amazon for parts for central vacuum systems or other toys. He will spend an hour copying every word on the Amazon page that describes the item that he thinks we need to order. Sometimes we will find these papers in our mailbox, because Jason thinks Santa will receive them and he will get his request at Christmas. He still believes in Santa because he has no reason not to. It doesn't even make sense to him when we tell him there is no Santa. I don't think he will ever stop making his lists for Santa and that is ok. I remember back when I still believed in Santa and it was such a fun time, so the fact that my giant child still believes is ok with me.

We do our best to make sure the computers are always signed out of Amazon, because Jason has actually ordered vacuum parts before. Even if we catch it a few minutes after he has ordered, it still ships and we have to deal with returning it. Once Jason had the entire central vacuum system saved in his cart. The cost was over $2000 for that one. Luckily, we caught it before he was able to place the order.

A lot of times people assume that people who have autism don't like to be around people. For Jason, that is not the case at all. Jason loves people, and people that know him, love him too. Jason can get so excited when he sees someone he likes, and he often will give them a big hug.

He gives the best hugs! He doesn't always play directly with his friends, but he likes to be near them. A good example of this is when we rent out the city pool for his birthday parties. He gets so excited knowing his friends are coming, but once they are there, he doesn't always interact with them in the pool, other than to occasionally splash them. That doesn't take away from the fact that he is happy that they are there.

Over the past year and a half, Jason has been developing a new friendship with a boy named Logan, who is a few years younger. The interesting thing about Logan is that he and Jason have a similar build and almost look like they could be brothers. They have a lot of the same mannerisms and just seemed to have hit it off right away. He is one of the very few kids we've ever had over for a play date, because for once, Jason has actually found someone that he really clicks with. Just recently, both of them spent a week at a summer camp for kids with special needs. They had their beds right next to each other and were pretty much inseparable the entire week.

Jason also loves his friends from school. It's interesting to see him around them because he has developed his own language with some of them. If you ever want to see Jason's real personality, just get him around his classmates. He is so much more vocal and animated. Just recently Jason's teachers rounded up most of his classmates over summer break to take them out to McDonalds for lunch. When Ms. V came to the door to pick him up, Jason instantly started talking and was so excited. Jason, along with many of his friends get bored when school is out on break. As much as I do my best to keep him busy, he is always happiest when he is back with his classmates.

Speaking of summer, Jason usually goes swimming almost every day, not only in the summer but year-round. There are about two months of the year that the pool is just too cold to go in, so during those times, Jason will just go in our hot tub. This boy who used to be terrified to go near the pool, now loves to be in it. It really is one of the activities where he can interact more with kids. Today we are invited to go to a new friend's pool on the island. Jason will get to meet her 4-year-old grandson and I'm pretty sure he's going to have a great time.

As much as I sometimes get a little sad to know Jason won't be following the same path of other kids that he has gone to school with, I do know that he has had a positive impact on a lot of them. It's really heartwarming to see so many of his classmates greet him whenever they see him. At his high school graduation, his senior class donated $500 of money they had raised to our Capable Kids Foundation. It was truly a full circle moment. Jason and his classmates had left such an impression on their peers, that those peers donated their senior class funds to help us continue our programs for kids with disabilities.

If that doesn't give you hope for this next generation of kids, I don't know what else would.

There is so much more to Jason to just sum up in a short chapter, but I want you to understand that although autism definitely affects Jason in his every-day life, it has not taken away from the very special and loving person that he has grown up to be. We have raised three kids now into adulthood and they are all very different. There is a silver lining for us, having a son like Jason, and that is that I get to avoid the empty nest syndrome that some of my friends go through. Honestly, it's been difficult enough having my oldest two kids gone most of the time, I can't imagine having Jason leave home too. Life would not be the same without him here to liven it up for us.

Chapter 23

The story continues

Thanks to my beautiful son Jason, my entire world has changed. As much as I wish he didn't have to go through all the struggles that he does, I realize that God can use his struggles to create a better world for those around us. I am so thankful at this point in my journey with Jason, to be able to turn something that was difficult, into something beautiful and meaningful. I know Jason has impacted my family in ways we can't describe, and, because of it we are all better off.

As a parent of a special- needs child, life changes a lot. In the earlier years of being a mom, I organized Bunco groups and girl's nights out for me and my friends. I used to also do play dates with the kids, teach Sunday school, and help out whenever I could, but that just got to be too much. I still have many friends who I keep in touch with, but honestly, it's not as easy to keep up with those friendships as it used to be. My focus has changed through the years, and although I occasionally do still get a rare night hanging out with friends, it's fewer and farther between. I spend a lot of time planning and working for things that I am passionate about, and when I'm not doing that, I really do enjoy just hanging out and watching a movie with my best friend, my husband Scott.

I may not have mentioned Scott that much, but it truly is because of him that I am able to be there for Jason and all the other kids, that I love doing events and activities for. I thank God for his—what seems at times—endless energy, to roughhouse with Jason in the pool or go with him on scooter rides around the neighborhood. I also make sure he has time to go do what he loves, which is kiteboarding. We are fortunate to be within a short bike ride of the bay, so if it's windy, he usually will head out for an hour or two on the water.

There are two other extremely important people who are part of our journey, and those are my parents. They usually have Jason at their house at least one night a week so we get a little break. They also are always there to help get Jason off the bus or off to school in the morning, if I have to go somewhere early, not to mention they are the ones who usually watch Jason when Scott and I go on vacation. At this point, Jason isn't too difficult to care for, but he makes a mess in no time flat, and even though he may not speak a lot, he definitely is not quiet.

I know most kids at the age of 18 don't need round the clock supervision, but Jason at this point definitely still needs someone to watch him. He's great at entertaining himself, but he can very quickly do something to put his life at risk, like causing a fire in the microwave or walking in front of a moving vehicle. He also had been known to get ahold of hair clippers and cut his own hair.

For most people, their kids grow up and move on and Jason is still is here at home, playing with his trains and sidewalk chalk. It was definitely a little easier when Jason's brother and sister still lived at home. For now, we are adjusting to this next chapter of our life.

Now that Jason has officially graduated, he can still attend school through the age of 21, where he will focus on learning job skills and also more life skills. In some ways Jason is a typical teenager; he loves listening to music on his iPad. We have bought him countless sets of headphones, but he has broken every set, so we basically get to listen to the music that he listens to. Occasionally, I catch him singing along and hearing his voice always makes me smile.

Jason also pays attention when he sees a pretty girl. I don't know if he'll ever be at the point in his life where he might have a girlfriend and that always makes me a little sad. Jason isn't sad though, for the most part, he is a happy kid. At the end of the day, I know we all hope and pray for our kids to be happy and healthy, so for that I am truly thankful.

I started writing our story by saying I was just a mom, and that is still true. For all of us moms out there, I wanted to share my journey with Jason to show you just what one mom with a special-needs child can do. We don't need to sit at home and feel sorry for the life our child isn't having, instead we can do what we can, to give our kids the opportunity to experience life in the way that works for them.

As for the name of our story, Jason helped me come up with it. There came a point in our life that I felt like we had been through many dark times and storms, when one day, I was driving in the car with Jason and there was a rainbow off in the distance. Jason got all excited and said "mom, rainbow!". It was at that moment that I realized we had survived so many storms in our life, and in the process, we were able to unexpectedly run into the rainbow. Our struggles had truly led us to where we are right now, and we are blessed beyond measure! Life may not always go the way we would like, but in the end, I truly hope that everyone gets to the point, that they run into their own rainbow and see the beauty that their unexpected journey has brought them.

Thank you for taking the time to read about our journey! There are so many more details of what has gone on through the years, but I did my best to share some of the information that I find myself sharing repeatedly in conversations with other families who are navigating the path of their own journey with their children. I can only hope and pray that your child will open up your eyes to the beautiful gifts that only they can bring into this world.

Afterword 2020

Just over a year ago, I sat down to write our story. I never expected it would take me an entire year to get through multiple edits, but now here we are. Thank you to my good friend Jessica Hedrick for doing my first edit. I never realized how often I did not use commas until that edit! Thanks to my mom for the second read through and suggestions. My third and final edit was done by a former classmate of our oldest son Dylan. Her name is Alana Hernandez and she writes for a local newspaper here in the valley. She was in the process of editing this book, when COVID-19 started emerging. As you can imagine, she suddenly found herself much busier than she ever expected to be. Thankfully though, she was able to finish editing and I had one more read through, before getting to this point.

This last year has brought with it many changes. It's safe to say, our world has completely changed since I finished the last chapter of this book. As Jason has gotten older, my focus has changed from creating events, to instead build life skills. I want to help him and others like him as they transition into adulthood.

I hadn't planned on making any major changes, but God definitely had different plans. The end of January this year, I made the decision to step down from my role as a full-time volunteer and Program Director for Capable Kids Foundation Lower Valley. As with all things in life, there is a season and my season had come to an end. There is a saying that goes "when God closes a door, he always opens a window." That was definitely true in my case, but instead of just opening a window, He opened more like an entire garage door! No sooner did I realize it was time to leave my former position, than I was offered a position with another nonprofit organization called BiG Heroes, Inc.

I had been following BiG Heroes on Facebook for a while and absolutely loved what they were accomplishing for young adults with disabilities. They provided continued education, life skills and job skills training once students with disabilities graduated from High School. I met their Executive Director, Martha Gonzalez, in the early part of 2019 and I loved that she had the same love for our special needs community as I do. She even had her students help fill 3,000 Easter Eggs for one of the events I put on for our kids in 2019. This was the place that I hoped Jason would be able to go to once he aged out of the high school at age 21.

I was very excited to join the team, and for the first time in my life, I am even being paid a small salary to do what I love. I had a very busy six weeks on the job before our Spring Break (in the middle of March). I'm sure I don't have to explain much of what came next, because I don't think anyone on the planet could escape being affected by the Corona Virus. As with every school in our state and most of the country, BiG Heroes had to stay closed for safety reasons.

Our staff didn't miss a beat though, because we knew how important our program was to our students. The first Tuesday after Spring Break, we started a Distance Learning program for BiG Heroes. Jason, started participating with our online program and something incredible occurred. Jason made it very clear to me that he does not want to go back to High School, and he only wants to go to BiG Heroes. To be honest, this came as a complete shock to me because he loved going to school and seeing all his friends. He also loved riding the school bus. I explained to him that if he went to BiG Heroes, everything would be different and he made it very clear that he was ready.

As of right now, we still haven't reopened, but I am doing a lot of work remotely and going into our center a couple times a week. Jason is with me full time now, which means, for the most part, he goes where I go. Even though our students aren't back yet, Jason loves going to BiG Heroes already and he is always asking when "the kids" will be joining him. He has met many of them over our weekly Zoom calls. It is amazing to me how ready he was for this change, even though I was not.

As crazy as things are in the world at the moment, I see the blessings that are still all around me. Jason continues to lead me in new directions and in doing so, I hope to grow our BiG Heroes program so that all young adults who have the desire to continue learning, will have the opportunity.

Another exciting opportunity came to fruition at the end of 2019. Two of the former Executive Directors that I worked with previously, Esmeralda Leal and Evelyn Cano and I, founded a Disability Chamber of Commerce. It's the fourth such chamber in the nation and definitely much needed. Our Disability Chamber of Commerce RGV is also a nonprofit and we will be working with businesses to help create more job opportunities for individuals with disabilities. It still blows my mind that not only am I able to have a part of helping with continuing education, but also job creation. Talk about God having a plan!

As difficult as all these recent changes have been for many, I know that my experiences over the years—from being a special needs parent—have definitely prepared me to know that life doesn't always go as planned. Just like our journey here at home, it's not always easy, but we have faith that through it all, God is doing his work. All we have to do is trust His plan and keep finding our rainbows.

Thank you for allowing me to share our story with you! I am truly honored that you took the time to read it and encourage you to share with other parents out there. May God bless you and your family as you continue on your own unique journey.

References

To find out more about putting your child on the Medicaid Waiver waiting list in South Texas, please call Tropical Behavioral Heath at 800-831-1233

Books I recommend reading for more information regarding vaccines include:

Dissolving Illusions: Disease, Vaccines, and the Forgotten History, Roman Bystianyk and Suzanne Humphries

The Autism Vaccine: The Story of Modern Medicine's Greatest Tragedy, Forrest Maready

The Virus and the Vaccine, Debbie Bookchin and Jim Schumaker

Made in the USA
Columbia, SC
23 August 2020